# Marie Catherine Laveau: Historical Narrative and Genealogy

Kenneth Dantzler-Corbin

# DEDICATION

This book is dedicated to the many descendants of Marie Catherine Laveau.

# Table of Contents

# ACKNOWLEDGMENTS

I would like to acknowledge all of my ancestors and living relatives who encouraged me to write about Marie Catherine Laveau.

# Chapter 1 Marie Catherine Laveau

Marie Catherine Laveau (September 10, 1801–June 15, 1881) was a Louisiana Creole practitioner of Voodoo, herbalist, and midwife in New Orleans. Her daughter, Marie Laveau II, (1827–c. 1862) practiced rootwork, conjured Native American, and African spiritualism besides Louisiana Voodoo.[1] Historians recognize an alternate spelling of her title, Laveaux, as being from the original spelling that is French.[2]

A picture of Marie Catherine Laveau

---

[1] "Marie Laveau | Biography & Facts | Britannica.
https://www.britannica.com/biography/Marie-Laveau. Accessed 15 Aug. 2020.
[2] "Marie Laveau | Biography & Facts | Britannica.
https://www.britannica.com/biography/Marie-Laveau. Accessed 15 Aug. 2020.

## Prior life

Historical documents suggested that Marie Laveau was born a woman free of colonial New Orleans (today's French Quarter), Louisiana (New France) on Thursday, September 10, 1801.[3] She was the biological child of Charles Trudeau, a mulatto grocery store owner, and son of Charles Laveau Trudeau, an assessor and legislator.[4] Marie's mother was Marguerite Henry (known as Marguerite D'Arcantel), a free woman of color of Choctaw Native American, African, and descent that is French. Marie's Parents were free people of color.[5]

On August 4, 1819, she wedded Jacques Paris (called Jacques Santiago in Spanish documents), a Quadroon, an individual one-quarter black by descent, Freeman of color who had fled being a refugee from the Haitian Revolution within the former French colony of Saint-Domingue.[6] They preserved their wedding certificate into the St. Louis Cathedral in New Orleans.[7]

Father Antonio de Sedella, the Capuchin priest, did the wedding mass known as Pere Antoine. Jacques was part White and Creoles of Color immigration of immigrants to New Orleans in 1809, from the Haitian Revolution of 1791-1804.[8]

Marie and Jacques had two daughters, Felicite, in 1817, and Angele in

---

[3] "The Story of French New Orleans History of a Creole City.
https://t7.smoloblvetlab.ru/3. Accessed 15 Aug. 2020.

[4] "Marie Laveau The Voodoo Queen of New Orleans - Naked .... 20 Sep. 2015,
http://www.historynaked.com/marie-laveau-voodoo-queen-new-orleans/.
Accessed 15 Aug. 2020.

[5] "Marie Laveau – WRSP - World Religions and Spirituality Project. 27 Oct. 2017,
https://wrldrels.org/2017/10/27/marie-laveau/. Accessed 15 Aug. 2020.

[6] "Negotiating Race and Status in Senegal, Saint Domingue ....
http://www.columbia.edu/~pf3/rossignol.pdf. Accessed 15 Aug. 2020.

[7] "slaveholding free women of color in antebellum New Orleans ....
https://digitalcommons.lsu.edu/cgi/viewcontent.cgi?article=4071&context=gradschool_dissertations. Accessed 15 Aug. 2020.

[8] "Free women of color and slaveholding in New Orleans, 1810 ....
https://digitalcommons.lsu.edu/cgi/viewcontent.cgi?article=4012&context=gradschool_theses. Accessed 15 Aug. 2020.

1820. Marie and Jacques vanished from the chronicles in the 1820s census records. Jacques Santiago Paris worked as a carpenter. The census taker recorded the death of Jacques Paris in 1820.[9]

## Private Life

Marie Catherine Laveau was the offspring of a mulatto man and a multiracial female. Marie Laveau was a free female of the color of African, Native American, and French descent. Laveau's only two young children to survive into adulthood were baby girls. The elder christened Marie Eucharist Eloise Laveau (1827–1862), the next daughter as Marie Philomene Glapion (1836–1897).[10]

Soon after the documented death of her husband, she entered a domestic relationship with Christophe Dominick Duminy de Glapion, an aristocrat of French descent, with whom she stayed until his passing in 1855. Scholars documented them to have had 15 young children (it is not clear if that includes children and grandchildren).

Christophe and Marie had seven children under birth and baptismal documents. They were François-Auguste Glapion Felicite Paris, Marie-Louise "Caroline" Glapion, Marie-Philomene Glapion, Marie-Angelie Paris, Celestin Albert Glapion, Arcange Glapion, and Marie-Heloise Eucharist Glapion.

There is a record shown that Marie had children by Francois Augustin. The children listed are Lorenzo Augustin, Marie Henriette Augustin, Francesca Augustin, Joseph Augustin, Felix Augustin, Francois Augustin, and Marie Carene Augustin.[11]

Scholars confirmed Marie Laveau to have owned at least seven slaves during her lifetime.

---

[9] "The House on Bayou Road: Atlantic Creole Networks in ... - jstor. https://www.jstor.org/stable/44308570. Accessed 15 Aug. 2020.
[10] "The House on Bayou Road: Atlantic Creole Networks in ... - jstor. https://www.jstor.org/stable/44308570. Accessed 15 Aug. 2020.
[11] "Haitians: A People on the Move. Haitian Cultural Heritage .... https://files.eric.ed.gov/fulltext/ED416263.pdf. Accessed 15 Aug. 2020.

## Career

Marie Laveau was a committed practitioner of Voodoo and a healer and herbalist. "they claimed Laveau to have ventured the streets as she possessed them," said one New Orleans boy who went to a function at St. John's. Her daughter, Marie Laveau II, showed more theatrical performance rubrics by supporting community activities (like welcoming guests to St. John's Eve ceremonies on Bayou St. John). They do not understand which (if either) had done to build the voodoo queen standing.[12]

Marie Laveau began a beauty shop where she was a hairdresser for the affluent households of New Orleans.[13] Of Laveau's magical occupation, there was little that scholars corroborated, including irrespective of whether she possessed a serpent she called Zombi after an African god.[14]

Whether the supernatural part of her charming blended Roman Catholic saints using African spirits and Native American Spiritualism or her divinations, she had a community of informants she developed even though operating as a hairdresser in separate white households.[15] She succeeded at getting valuable information on her affluent clients by instilling fear in their servants, with whom she both compensated and healed of strange illnesses.[16]

Some recognized Laveau as a feminine faith-based leader and community

---

[12] "The Black Auxiliary Troops of King Carlos IV - Vanderbilt's .... 17 May. 2015, https://etd.library.vanderbilt.edu/available/etd-05172015-181542/unrestricted/MiriamMartinErickson.pdf. Accessed 15 Aug. 2020.

[13] "Marie laveau. https://divansale.com/wmr6qzd/marie-laveau.html. Accessed 15 Aug. 2020.

[14] "Marie laveau. https://divansale.com/wmr6qzd/marie-laveau.html. Accessed 15 Aug. 2020.

[15] "Marie laveau. https://divansale.com/wmr6qzd/marie-laveau.html. Accessed 15 Aug. 2020.

[16] "Marie laveau. https://divansale.com/wmr6qzd/marie-laveau.html. Accessed 15 Aug. 2020.

activist.

## Demise

Plaque at the tomb of Louisiana Voodoo Queen, Marie Laveau

Marie Catherine Laveau Paris Glapion died June 15, 1881, aged 79.[17] The various spellings of her family name result from different females with a similar name in New Orleans.[18]

On June 17, 1881, they revealed in the Daily Picayune that Marie Laveau died quietly in her residence. Based on the Louisiana Writers Project, her funeral service was luxurious and visited by various viewers, including patrons of the white professional. Oral practice says a few people in town viewed her at once after her intended death.[19]

---

[17] "Marie Glapion - Historical records and family trees - MyHeritage. https://www.myheritage.com/names/marie_glapion. Accessed 15 Aug. 2020.
[18] "Marie Glapion - Historical records and family trees - MyHeritage. https://www.myheritage.com/names/marie_glapion. Accessed 15 Aug. 2020.
[19] "Marie Catherine Laveau, Voodoo Priestess (c.1801 - c.1881 .... 13 Apr. 2020, https://www.geni.com/people/Marie-Laveau-Voodoo-Priestess/6000000012337864987. Accessed 15 Aug. 2020.

At least two of her children, she named Marie, after the French Catholic custom to have the first names of daughters as Marie, and males as Joseph, then each chooses the middle name as the common name. One of her daughters, known as Marie, resumed her position, with her identification, and kept on her enchanting practice, taking over as the queen soon before or at once after the first Marie's passing.[20]

---

[20] "Marie Laveau | New Orleans Voodoo Queen | History. https://ghostcitytours.com/new-orleans/marie-laveau/. Accessed 15 Aug. 2020.

# Chapter 2 Influence of voodoo leaders

Many superstitions held by Louisianians stem through the cult of Voodoo.[21] Voodoo was an animist belief that consecrates a cult to Loas (gods) also to the ancestors—the cult of ancestors constitutes a method of religious beliefs and rites that they people used principally to bolster the social system along with the dependence regarding the family—and at precisely the same time, voodoo spirits, protectors, deities, or forces of nature. Voodoo originated from Africa, explicitly using the Fon, Yoruba, and Ewe tribes. Geographically, those ethnic groups came from Ghana, Togo, Benin, and Nigeria. Significantly more than a religion or a cult of death, voodoo played an essential role in everyday life through the symbolization regarding the African traditions when it comes to Haitian people. Voodoo was not even close to traditional worship but evolved differently from one region to a higher.[22] The people imported voodoo rites and charms into the location with the initial delivery of slaves from Africa to the colony of Louisiana in 1718, the season the city of New Orleans was founded.[23] The initial cargo of slaves arrived through the Guinea coast of Africa, and succeeding deliveries came through the French colonies of Martinique, Guadaloupe, and Santo Domingo, that have been hotbeds of voodooism.[24]

The people from Haiti brought the voodoo cult together with them. Vodou, an Afro-Haitian religion, is a worldview encompassing philosophy, medicine, justice, and religion. Its fundamental principle is the fact that all things are spirit. Humans are spirits who inhabit the visible world. The unseen world has a lwa (spirits), mystè (mysteries), anvizib (the invisible),

---

[21] "Louisiana voodoo and superstitions related to health.. https://www.ncbi.nlm.nih.gov/pmc/articles/PMC1937133/. Accessed 27 Aug. 2020.
[22] Voodoo - rituals, world, burial, body, life, beliefs, time .... http://www.deathreference.com/Vi-Z/Voodoo.html
[23] "JULIE YVONNE WEBB, RN, MS Hyg. Miss Webb ... - CDC stacks. https://stacks.cdc.gov/view/cdc/62808/cdc_62808_DS1.pdf?. Accessed 27 Aug. 2020.
[24] "The Catholic Voodoo Queen and the Demonization of New .... https://digitalcommons.chapman.edu/cgi/viewcontent.cgi?article=1106&context=vocesnovae. Accessed 27 Aug. 2020.

zanj (angels), in addition to spirits of ancestors together with recently deceased. Individuals considered the spirits to live in a mythic land called Ginen, a cosmic "Africa." The God of the Christian Bible is the creator of both the universe and spirits; the spirits were created by God to assist in governing humanity in the natural world. The foundation about the Haitian cult of voudon or voudu traced to Dahomey in West Africa.[25]

The Dahomean word "vodu" designates the polytheistic deities worshipped by Dahomeans. Its magic, sorcery, and witchcraft are secondary to, or byproducts of, Voodoo as a religious faith. [26]In Louisiana, Africans continued their belief in fetishes and their cult regarding the great serpent god.[27] Some cultists professed to own supernatural powers to accomplish things ordinary people cannot do, and so received the terrified respect of these people.[28] The belief in Voodoo spread to white people, and years talk of voodoo influences was common. [29]

Some understood that voodoo queens, influential female practitioners of the religious beliefs, used substantial power in their networks and had the position of trust for many of the formal religious meetings and religious ceremony dances.[30] These attracted crowds of hundreds and thousands of people. They made a living through the attempting to sell and administering amulets, or "gris-gris" talismans, and phenomenal powders, and invocations, and talismans that guaranteed to "cure illnesses, grant

[25] "Haitian Immigration to Louisiana in the Eighteenth ... - AAME :. http://www.inmotionaame.org/texts/viewer.cfm?id=5_000T. Accessed 27 Aug. 2020.
[26] "Haitian Immigration to Louisiana in the Eighteenth ... - AAME :. http://www.inmotionaame.org/texts/viewer.cfm?id=5_000T. Accessed 27 Aug. 2020.
[27] "Political and Economic History of Haiti - San Jose State .... https://www.sjsu.edu/faculty/watkins/haiti.htm. Accessed 27 Aug. 2020.
[28] "Haitian Revolution | Causes, Summary, & Facts | Britannica. https://www.britannica.com/topic/Haitian-Revolution. Accessed 27 Aug. 2020.
[29] "Haitian Immigration : Eighteenth and Nineteenth Centuries. http://www.inmotionaame.org/print.cfm?migration=5. Accessed 27 Aug. 2020.
[30] "Chapter 13: Religion (ANTH 1010) Flashcards | Quizlet. https://quizlet.com/290432641/chapter-13-religion-anth-1010-flash-cards/. Accessed 15 Aug. 2020.

desires, and confuse or destroy one's opponents.[31]

Their energy and impact were widespread and incontestable. Journalists, judges, thieves, and residents recognized alike. These women of African and Creole descent surfaced as decisive leadership in a society that upheld an oppressive slave authority and a dichotomy of independence between blacks and whites. The people sensed their influence in black and white circles alike, because of the prior history of the location, in which "a shortage of white women lead in a high number of interracial liaisons.[32]

As in other French colonial communities, a class of free people of color strengthened whom they provided specified privileges and, in New Orleans, gained real estate and education. Free women of color had an impact on those who were spiritual leaders. The religious practices in West and middle Africa, from where many voodoo practices originated, supplied for women to exercise extraordinary capability.[33]

Marie Laveau midst the fifteen "voodoo queens" in areas scattered around 19th-century New Orleans, some knew Marie Laveau as "the Voodoo Queen," the most eminent and useful of these all. Her spiritual rite on the Coast of Lake Pontchartrain on St. John's Eve in 1874 attracted some 12,000 black and white New Orleanians.[34]

Haitian Blacks came in the 18th century and the beginning of the 19th century to New Orleans. The French came from Santo Domingo by slave uprisings that resulted in the establishment of the Haitian Republic.[35] The

[31] "Chapter 13: Religion (ANTH 1010) Flashcards | Quizlet.
https://quizlet.com/290432641/chapter-13-religion-anth-1010-flash-cards/.
Accessed 15 Aug. 2020.
[32] "American History Week 5 Flashcards | Quizlet.
https://quizlet.com/339148012/american-history-week-5-flash-cards/.
Accessed 15 Aug. 2020.
[33] "Midterm essay for anthropology course | Social Science ....
https://www.homeworkmarket.com/files/mythritualmysticismbook-pdf-5148409. Accessed 15 Aug. 2020.
[34] "Voodoo priestess new orleans. http://mcbpc20088.nichost.ru/rsvc/voodoo-priestess-new-orleans.html. Accessed 15 Aug. 2020.
[35] "Haitian Revolution | Causes, Summary, & Facts | Britannica.
https://www.britannica.com/topic/Haitian-Revolution. Accessed 27 Aug. 2020.

people brought the voodoo cult together with them.

Scholars traced the foundation about the Haitian cult of voudon or voudu traced to Dahomey in West Africa.[36] The Dahomean word "voodoo" designates the polytheistic deities worshipped by Dahomeans.[37] Its magic, sorcery, and witchery are supplementary to, or byproducts of, Voodoo as a religious faith.[38]

In Louisiana, Africans sustained their belief in fetishes and their cult regarding the great serpent god.[39] Some cultists professed to own supernatural powers to accomplish things ordinary people cannot do, and so received the terrified respect of these people.[40]

The belief in Voodoo extended to white people. The people spread the influence of voodoo in New Orleans. Even though the development of the cult in Louisiana seemed slow, Governor Bernardo de Galvez prohibited further imports of slaves in 1782 since voodooism had become such a possible menace.[41] "They are way too much fond of voudouism and then make the lives regarding the citizens unsafe. [42]

The United States of America in the 1800s acquired the Louisiana terrain; at the very least 5,000 refugee Africans, free and slave, found their way to

---

[36] "Haitian Revolution | Causes, Summary, & Facts | Britannica.
https://www.britannica.com/topic/Haitian-Revolution. Accessed 27 Aug. 2020.
[37] "Religion, History and the Supreme Gods of Africa: A ... - jstor.
https://www.jstor.org/stable/1581452. Accessed 27 Aug. 2020.
[38] "Voodoo dictionary definition | voodoo defined - YourDictionary.
https://www.yourdictionary.com/voodoo. Accessed 27 Aug. 2020.
[39] "voodoo in louisiana - Core.
https://core.ac.uk/download/pdf/295552849.pdf. Accessed 27 Aug. 2020.
[40] "Pentecostalism and Witchcraft.
https://link.springer.com/content/pdf/10.1007%2F978-3-319-56068-7.pdf.
Accessed 27 Aug. 2020.
[41] "Slavery in Spanish Colonial Louisiana | 64 Parishes.
https://64parishes.org/entry/slavery-in-spanish-colonial-louisiana. Accessed 27 Aug. 2020.
[42] "Slavery in Spanish Colonial Louisiana | 64 Parishes.
https://64parishes.org/entry/slavery-in-spanish-colonial-louisiana. Accessed 27 Aug. 2020.

New Orleans between 1806 and 1810.[43] The introduction of voodooism as a proper aspect in the lives of Louisiana Creoles began with this specific influx. [44]

Some stated that politicians, lawyers, people in business, wealthy planters—all came to her to consult before one can make a significant economic or business-related decision. She saw the poor and enslaved.[45]

Although her help seemed non-discriminatory, she could have favored enslaved servants: Her many "influential, affluent customers...runaway slaves...credited their effective escapes to Laveaux's powerful charms". Once the news of her abilities spread, she dominated one other Voodoo leader of New Orleans. A Catholic, Laveau, invigorated her followers to attend Catholic Mass. Her impact contributed to the use of Catholic methods into the Voodoo belief system. One remembered Marie Laveau for her ability and compassion for the less fortunate.[46]

Laveau gained an impact over her clientele by her time task as being a hairdresser, which affords her knowledge that is intimate of gossip in town. Her clients found her buying voodoo dolls, potions, gris-gris bags. Her impact continued in the city. Into the twenty-first century, her gravesite within the earliest cemetery is a famous tourist attraction; believers of Voodoo offered gifts.[47]

Down the street of the cemetery where they buried Laveau, individuals left offerings of lb. dessert towards the statue of Saint Expedite; individuals

[43] "Bernardo de Galvez | 64 Parishes. https://64parishes.org/entry/bernardo-de-glvez. Accessed 27 Aug. 2020.
[44] "The Slave Trade and the Ethnic Diversity of Louisiana's ... - jstor. https://www.jstor.org/stable/4233285. Accessed 27 Aug. 2020.
[45] "What Is Louisiana Voodoo Really All About Anyway?. 18 Jul. 2016, https://wheninyourstate.com/louisiana/what-is-that-voodoo-that-you-do/. Accessed 15 Aug. 2020.
[46] "What Is Louisiana Voodoo Really All About Anyway?. 18 Jul. 2016, https://wheninyourstate.com/louisiana/what-is-that-voodoo-that-you-do/. Accessed 15 Aug. 2020.
[47] "What Is Louisiana Voodoo Really All About Anyway?. 18 Jul. 2016, https://wheninyourstate.com/louisiana/what-is-that-voodoo-that-you-do/. Accessed 15 Aug. 2020.

considered these offerings would favor the Voodoo queen. Saint Expedite stands for the character standing between life and death. The chapel where the statue stands, some used only for holding funerals. Marie Laveau continued to be a figure central to Voodoo and New Orleans culture. Gamblers shout her name whenever dice that are throwing, and they told multiple stories of sightings of the Voodoo queen.[48]

[48] "New Orleans City Guide 1938 - NOLA Pyrate Week. https://nolapyrateweek.com/wp-content/uploads/New_Orleans_City_Guide_1938.pdf. Accessed 15 Aug. 2020.

# Chapter 3 Louisiana Creole People of Color

Louisiana Creole people (French: Creoles de la Louisiane, Spanish: Criollos de Louisiana) are persons descended through the inhabitants of colonial Louisiana through the period of both French and Spanish rule. Louisiana Creoles share social ties such as the traditional use of the French, Spanish, and Louisiana Creole languages and the competent practice of Catholicism.[49]

French settlers used the definition of Créole to tell apart people born in Louisiana from those born within the country or elsewhere.[50] Like in many other colonial communities around the world, Creole was a term used to suggest those that were "native-born," or native-born Europeans like the French and Spanish.[51] It came into existence applied to African-descended slaves and Native Americans who were born in Louisiana.[52]

The phrase is not a racial label, and people of European descent, African descent, or of any mixture (including Native American admixture) may recognize Creoles.[53] Beginning with the native-born children of the French, and native-born slaves that are African, 'Creole' came into existence used to explain Louisiana-born people to differentiate them from European immigrants and brought in slaves.[54]

---

[49] "Creoles | Encyclopedia.com. https://www.encyclopedia.com/social-sciences-and-law/anthropology-and-archaeology/people/creoles. Accessed 15 Aug. 2020.

[50] "Creoles - History, The first creoles in america, Acculturation .... https://www.everyculture.com/multi/Bu-Dr/Creoles.html. Accessed 27 Aug. 2020.

[51] "Creole | people | Britannica. https://www.britannica.com/topic/Creole. Accessed 27 Aug. 2020.

[52] "Creole in Louisiana - jstor. https://www.jstor.org/stable/27784777. Accessed 27 Aug. 2020.

[53] "What's the Difference Between Cajun and Creole? - TripSavvy. 28 May. 2019, https://www.tripsavvy.com/the-difference-between-cajun-and-creole-3961097. Accessed 27 Aug. 2020.

[54] "Creoles in Louisiana History – Seventh Coalition: History. 22 Jan. 2018, https://seventhcoalition.wordpress.com/2018/01/22/creoles-in-louisiana-history/. Accessed 15 Aug. 2020.

People of any mixture can identify as Creoles, and it is a misunderstanding that créolité—the quality of being Creole—suggests mixed racial ancestries.[55] Within the late nineteenth and 20th century, free people of color in Louisiana used the term Creole through the 20th century.[56] One historian described this era as the "Americanization of Creoles," in this American binary system. The system divided the racial Creoles into the ones that thought as white, among others, like black.[57]

The people used Créole as identification in the 1700s in Louisiana. Beginning in the early 1800s in Louisiana, following the USA gaining this territory within the Louisiana purchase, the word "Creole" undertook a far more meaning that is a political identity for those individuals of Latinate tradition. These are Catholic French speakers who had a culture that compared with the Protestant English-speaking and Anglo background of the new American settlers from the Upper Southern and the North.

In the early century 19th amid the Haitian Revolution, many refugees (both white and free persons of color from the Caribbean named Saint-Domingue (affranchis or gens de couleur libres) found its way to New Orleans, often bringing enslaved Africans using them. Therefore, many refugees arrived, and the town's population doubled. As they allowed more refugees in Louisiana, Haitian émigrés who had first visited Cuba arrived. These teams had substantial effects on the city and its culture. One half of the migrant white of Haiti settled in Louisiana, within the New Orleans area.[58]

Later, 19th-century immigrants who came to New Orleans were   Irish,

[55] "Contemporary Creoleness; or, The World in Pidginization? - jstor.
https://www.jstor.org/stable/10.1086/657257. Accessed 27 Aug. 2020.
[56] "The New Orleans Free People of Color and the Process of ....
https://scholarworks.wm.edu/cgi/viewcontent.cgi?article=6491&context=etd.
Accessed 27 Aug. 2020.
[57] "what does che mean in creole - Key Route Lofts #101.
http://keyroutelofts101.com/site/2a1ei.php?0c08af=what-does-che-mean-in-creole. Accessed 15 Aug. 2020.
[58] "Creole History in New Orleans - Visit New Orleans.
https://www.neworleans.com/things-to-do/multicultural/cultures/creoles/.
Accessed 15 Aug. 2020.

Germans, and Italians mixed into the groups that are Creole. All the recent immigrants had been Catholic.[59] There was a substantial German Creole group of complete German descent, centering about the communities of St. John the Baptist and St. Charles.[60] (It is for these colonizers that the Côte des Allemands, " The German Coast," is named.) Overall, many of these groups assimilated into the dominant French Creole culture, often adopting the language that is French traditions.[61]

Although Cajuns are presented in the century that is twenty-first a group distinct from the Creoles, many historic reports occur wherein individuals with Acadian surnames either self-identify or are identified by other people to be Creole.[62] Some nineteenth-century sources refer to "Acadian Creoles.[63] As people born in colonial Louisiana, they defined people of Acadian ancestry as Creole, and before the early-mid-20th century, the people considered Cajuns a subcategory of Louisiana Creole rather than a separate group.[64] Today some Louisianans who identify as Cajun reject relationships as Creole, while others may embrace race both identities.[65]

Creoles of French descent, counting those descended from the Acadians,

---

[59] "The National and Cultural Groups of New Orleans - Folklife in ....
http://www.louisianafolklife.org/lt/virtual_books/guide_to_state/NOGroups.ht
ml. Accessed 27 Aug. 2020.
[60] "The African American Experience in Louisiana. 15 May. 2012,
https://www.crt.state.la.us/Assets/OCD/hp/nationalregister/historic_contexts/
The_African_American_Experience_in_Louisiana.pdf. Accessed 27 Aug. 2020.
[61] "Social Classification in Creole Louisiana - jstor.
https://www.jstor.org/stable/643621. Accessed 15 Aug. 2020.
[62] "Racial and Ethnic Groups in the Gulf of Mexico Region: Cajuns.
https://www.lsuagcenter.com/~/media/system/c/1/6/3/c163dd4e4dfc692ac2
bd44060c49a0df/rr118racialandethnicgroupsinthegulfofmexicoregionc.pdf.
Accessed 27 Aug. 2020.
[63] "Download Creoles And Cajuns - myq-see.com or. http://lantved.myq-
see.com/509.html. Accessed 27 Aug. 2020.
[64] "Racial and Ethnic Groups in the Gulf of Mexico Region: Cajuns.
https://www.lsuagcenter.com/~/media/system/c/1/6/3/c163dd4e4dfc692ac2
bd44060c49a0df/rr118racialandethnicgroupsinthegulfofmexicoregionc.pdf.
Accessed 27 Aug. 2020.
[65] "Social Classification in Creole Louisiana - jstor.
https://www.jstor.org/stable/643621. Accessed 15 Aug. 2020.

have historically made all-white Creoles in Louisiana.[66] Louisiana Creoles are Catholic in religion. Through the nineteenth century, most Creoles spoke French and linked to French colonial culture.[67] The large Spanish Creole neighborhoods of Saint Bernard Parish and Galveztown spoke Spanish.[68] The Malagueños of New Iberia, most of these individuals spoke Spanish.[69] The Isleños and Malagueños were Spanish but live Louisiana-born of Creole heritage. Considering that the century is mid-20th, the full range of Spanish-speaking Creoles has declined, and only English-speaking individuals and few people under 80 years old spoke the Spanish language. They had kept social traditions through the Canary Islands; their immigrant ancestors came.[70]

Spanish Creoles, native languages of all groups, are Creole, whether French, Spanish, or German, declined over time to support the English spoken by most of the population. Distinct Louisiana's Creoles shaped the state's tradition, in the areas that are southern New Orleans and the plantation districts. The people called Louisiana the Creole State.[71]

While the classy Creole society of New Orleans, which highlighted on French Creoles, has gotten much attention, the Cane River vicinity in northwest Louisiana, populated by Creoles of color, developed a unique,

---

[66] "Connecting past to present: Louisiana cajuns and their sense .... 14 Feb. 2005, https://journals.openedition.org/nuevomundo/646. Accessed 27 Aug. 2020.
[67] "This is the difference between Cajun and Creole - 10Best. 20 Mar. 2018, https://www.10best.com/interests/food-culture/this-is-the-difference-between-cajun-and-creole/. Accessed 27 Aug. 2020.
[68] "History | Los Islenos Heritage and Cultural Society. https://www.losislenos.org/history/. Accessed 27 Aug. 2020.
[69] "Spanish legacy continues | People | iberianet.com. 22 Apr. 2018, https://www.iberianet.com/people/spanish-legacy-continues/article_85227f96-4509-11e8-b57a-7b134aea67cb.html. Accessed 27 Aug. 2020.
[70] "Creoles - History, The first creoles in america, Acculturation .... https://www.everyculture.com/multi/Bu-Dr/Creoles.html. Accessed 15 Aug. 2020.
[71] "Creole in Louisiana - jstor. https://www.jstor.org/stable/27784777. Accessed 15 Aug. 2020.

influential Creole culture. Other enclaves of Creole culture have now been in the South and Southwest Louisiana: Frilot Cove, Bois Mallet, Grand Marais, Palmetto, Lawtell, Soileau, yet others. These societies have had a long history of independence.[72]

New Orleans has received a significant historic populace of Creoles of color, friends that were free people of color, of blended European, African, and Native American descent. Another area where many creoles were, was around the River Parishes: St. Charles, St. James, and St. John. Many Creoles of German and French lineage settled there. We find many French Creoles within the greater New Orleans region, a seven parish-wide Creole area that is cultural Orleans, St. Bernard, Jefferson, Plaquemines, St. Charles, St. Tammany, and St. John the Baptist parishes. Avoyelles and Evangeline parishes in Acadiana likewise have significant French creole populations of French descent, referred to as French Creoles.[73]

## Ethnic blend and competition

Colonists described themselves and enslaved Black people who have been native-born as Creole, to distinguish them from recent arrivals from France and Spain along with Africa. Native People in America, such as the Creek people, intermixed with Creoles making three races present in the group that is ethnic.[74]

Like "Cajun," the term "Creole" is just a popular title used to explain cultures into the southern Louisiana area. One defines "Creole" as "native from a geographical area in which some use. Creoles felt the requirement to differentiate themselves from the influx of American and European immigrants coming into the area following the Louisiana Purchase of 1803. One used "Creole" as the heritage and traditions of the various people who settled Louisiana throughout the early French times that are

---

[72] "Spanish Colonial Louisiana | 64 Parishes. https://64parishes.org/entry/spanish-colonial-louisiana. Accessed 15 Aug. 2020.

[73] "Cajuns - 64 Parishes. https://64parishes.org/entry/cajuns. Accessed 15 Aug. 2020.

[74] "Slavery in the Colonial Louisiana Backcountry - jstor. https://www.jstor.org/stable/23074684. Accessed 15 Aug. 2020.

colonial. [75]

The incorporated Creole society in southern Louisiana includes influences from the Chitimacha, Houma, and other native tribes, enslaved West African, Spanish-speaking Isleños (Canary Islanders), and French-speaking Gens de Couleur Libres from the Caribbean besides the French Canadians. Being a shared group, mixed-race Creoles rapidly started to get training skills (many in New Orleans worked as craftsmen and artisans), organizations, and property. These were overwhelmingly Catholic, spoke Colonial French (although some spoke Louisiana Creole), and kept up many French social customs, changed by other parts of this ancestry and Louisiana tradition.[76]

They often marry the Creoles of Color among themselves to keep their class and culture that is social. The French-speaking mixed-race population came to become called "Creoles of color. Some said that "New Orleans individuals of color were far wealthier, better and competent than freed unmixed Black Creoles and Cajuns in Louisiana. Beneath the French and Spanish rulers, Louisiana developed a three-tiered society, like Haiti, Cuba, Brazil, Saint Lucia, Martinique, Guadeloupe, and other Latin colonies. This three-tiered society included white Creoles, a booming, educated band of mixed-race Creoles of European, African, and Native American descent, and the far bigger class of Black Creole and African slaves.[77]

The people guarded mixed-race Creoles of color (Gens de Couleur Libres) carefully. For legal reasons, they enjoyed all the same rights and privileges as white Creoles. [78] They might have challenged the legislation in court

---

[75] "Southern Folk Artist & Antiques Dealer/Collector: "Créole Soirée". 26 Jun. 2016, http://andrewhopkinsart.blogspot.com/2016/06/creole-soiree.html. Accessed 15 Aug. 2020.
[76] "The Portuguese and the Creole Indian Ocean Essays in Historical .... https://ii.metaldoor12.ru/141. Accessed 15 Aug. 2020.
[77] "Introduction: The Making and Unmaking of an Atlantic World .... https://www.oxfordhandbooks.com/view/10.1093/oxfordhb/9780199210879.001.0001/oxfordhb-9780199210879-e-1. Accessed 15 Aug. 2020.
[78] "The Free People of Color in Louisiana and St. Domingue: A .... https://www.jstor.org/stable/3786302. Accessed 15 Aug. 2020.

and won instances against white Creoles. They were property holders and created schools for their young ones. Most times, though, these different tiers saw themselves as one group, as other Iberoamericana and Francophone cultural teams did. The race did not play as central a role as it did the Anglo-American tradition: often, the race was not an issue, but household standing and wealth had been critical distinguishing factors in New Orleans and beyond.[79]

For five hundred years, America has been a land where people have sought, if not always found, freedom. They saw those that were successful as quintessential American heroes. While people commemorate freedom as the establishing tenet of the country, the great paradox concerning America was the continued presence and impact of slaveholding.

In the link of captivity and liberty were free people of color, the countless individuals of African lineage who surmounted incredible probabilities and survived free in the greatest improbable of places-the slave communities of the South, the Caribbean islands, plus Latin America in the eighteenth and previously nineteenth centuries. Several histories concerning NORTH AMERICA neglect to inform the story of resilient and exciting individuals.[80]

If most Americans at present were conscious that many black men and women, including Frederick Douglass to Harriet Tubman, could break free from southern area plantations and lived in freedom within the North prospered in areas where slavery was rooted that it took a war to abolish it. One place had been Louisiana.[81]

Throughout the antebellum time, Louisiana's free men and women of color treasured a full acknowledgment and wealth, a heritage of the state's French and Spanish pioneers. However, as the American Civil War approached, white culture progressively converted in opposition to these people. [82]

---

[79] "the education of louisiana's gens de couleur libres ... - Core. https://core.ac.uk/download/pdf/158321730.pdf. Accessed 15 Aug. 2020.
[80] "the education of louisiana's gens de couleur libres ... - Core. https://core.ac.uk/download/pdf/158321730.pdf. Accessed 15 Aug. 2020.
[81] "Free People of Color in the Spanish Atlantic Race and Citizenship .... https://v7.rodionblog.ru/58. Accessed 15 Aug. 2020.
[82] Free People of Color in Louisiana.

The majority intensely concentrated in New Orleans, countless worked as professionals and contractors. Significant numbers were within Baton Rouge, St. Landry Parish, and the Natchitoches area, where some were plantation owners and slaveholders. It was because of their efforts towards the artistry that Louisiana's free individuals of color came to become most readily known, with many showing themselves as authors, designers, and instrumentalists. Historians themselves began enjoying the sophistication of free African Americans and their importance to the comprehension not only of the history but the present day.[83]

The reality that free people of color, in the Southern states, in no means made it into the well-known story of American history is phenomenal considering their reputation was most likely one of the more talked-about dilemmas concerning the beginning half of the nineteenth century. Even where their quantities were limited, they made considerable advantages to the economic climates and cultures of the areas where they were living, and, as an organization, maintain a significant impact on governing policy and community viewpoint at the equivalent duration of growing polarization on the question of slavery.[84]

Neither did their narrative shed its relevancy once the abolishment of slavery had rendered all People in America lawfully free. Discrimination towards freedmen, blacks who experienced not have known slavery, and Creoles of Color in the postbellum South had an improved existence, where many about mixed-race culture had been able to "pass" in his or her new areas.

As the consequences of their exodus, southern black areas lacked accomplished leadership, men and women in business, role models, and social brokers at the duration when required. Those that remained, however, cooperated with other African Americans in the long struggle for civil rights.[85]

---

https://www.lib.lsu.edu/sites/all/files/sc/fpoc/history.html
[83] Free People of Color in Louisiana.
https://www.lib.lsu.edu/sites/all/files/sc/fpoc/history.html
[84] Free People of Color in Louisiana.
https://www.lib.lsu.edu/sites/all/files/sc/fpoc/history.html
[85] "The New Orleans Free People of Color and the Process of ....
https://scholarworks.wm.edu/cgi/viewcontent.cgi?article=6491&context=etd.
Accessed 15 Aug. 2020.

This project hopes to donate to the rediscovery of the "forgotten" people and their role within the state's racial, politically aware, economic, social, and                                         cultural                                          past.[86]

The background of free individuals of color in the Americas extends straight back to the starting of the period Exploration. The team of Christopher Columbus's first expedition included a free black deckhand. Juan Garrido, a black conquistador, voyage with Ponce de Leon and Pánfilo de Narváez in what was today the United States and Mexico, although Juan Valiente, a free black man coming from Cádiz, help lead the first Spanish excursion to Chile. Estéban de Dorantes, a black alárabe ("Arabized black"), protected the shipwrecked adventurer Álvar Núñez Cabeza de Vaca and their men from acute demise by posing as a shaman and convincing Native Americans to exchange their produce.[87]

Free individuals of color played a significant role inside Spain's " NEW WORLD " empire as soldiers, sailors, artisans, and laborers. Manumission, they granted slaves the right to purchase their freedom, had been customary in the Iberian Peninsula, and had been transplanted with the Spanish and Portuguese with their American colonies, offering rise to a significant and radiant populace of free individuals of color.[88]

The Roman Catholic religious beliefs, at minimum, dejected the captivity of individuals who had supported Christendom, ascribed to the progressive mindset of the Spanish and Portuguese regarding free men and women of color.[89]

In a few ways, the French had an identical outlook, imagining a society where a class was more important than competition and where everyone

[86] "The New Orleans Free People of Color and the Process of ....
https://scholarworks.wm.edu/cgi/viewcontent.cgi?article=6491&context=etd. Accessed 15 Aug. 2020.
[87] "The African American heritage of Florida.
https://ufdc.ufl.edu/AA00061985/00001. Accessed 15 Aug. 2020.
[88] "A Little History of the United States - REPUBLIC OF CALLAMARI.
https://republicofcallamari.weebly.com/uploads/3/8/0/7/38076783/a_little_hi story_of_the_united_states.pdf. Accessed 15 Aug. 2020.
[89] "Facts-on-File-Atlas-of-Hispanic-American-History.pdf.
https://saalimited.com/PDFS/files/1.%20P.D.F.'s/Facts-on-File-Atlas-of-Hispanic-American-History.pdf. Accessed 15 Aug. 2020.

was eligible for fair treatment, stating that the church christened them into the Catholic tradition. For all its austerity, the French Code Noir, adopted in 1685, integrated articles safeguarding the rights of freed slaves, which were the same as those of whites, with the exception that they might not vote, hold public office, or marry a white individual. While the French, Spanish, and Portuguese codes viewed slaves and free blacks less harshly and provided more excellent legal security than did Protestant countries, localized problems such as slave revolts and the duration of the territories from fundamental administrative regulation perhaps more directly involved their encounters.

The French were furthermore more understanding of racial mixing, in sparsely settled boundary communities such as Louisiana, where there have been dramatically fewer white females than males. At the same duration, they created sophisticated color classes to determine the outcomes of that mixing.[90]

In the English territories, individuals of African lineage, free or not, encountered extreme societal and legal constraints.[91] Race, for the British, was as imperative as a class. A lot of the English colonies in North America, and the Caribbean, passed formal black codes between the 1670s and 1750s. Slaves there had minimal legal standing, and freed slaves and freeborn Africans had few civil rights. Men and women had to transport "freedom documents" anywhere they moved, as verification of their reputation, and those with no documents ran the danger of becoming re-enslaved.[92]

## Black Codes and Pig Laws

Shortly after the Civil War concluded, Southern states introduced "black codes," which allowed African Americans some legal rights, such as

---

[90] "the european - World history.
http://www.worldhistory.biz/download567/TheAmericanIndians-TheEuropeanChallenge(History%20Ebook)_worldhistory.biz.pdf. Accessed 15 Aug. 2020.
[91] Free People of Color in Louisiana.
https://www.lib.lsu.edu/sites/all/files/sc/fpoc/history.html
[92] "A Companion to Latin American History - Wiley Online Library.
https://onlinelibrary.wiley.com/doi/pdf/10.1002/9781444391633. Accessed 15 Aug. 2020.

legalized matrimony, possession of the real estate, and restricted accessibility to the process of law. However, they denied them the right to testify against whites, to serve injuries or within state militias, vote, or take up a job minus the approval of the prior employer. These rules had been all repealed in 1866 when Reconstruction started.[93]

Following the failure of Reconstruction inside 1877, and whites removed black men from political workplaces, Southern states once again enacted some laws designed to circumscribe the existence of African Americans. Harsh agreement laws and regulations penalized anyone wanting to leave employment. "Pig Laws and regulations" unfairly penalized deficient African Americans for offenses such as stealing a plantation pet.

The laws pertained to Blacks for vagrancy (a state of living homeless and destitute) or becoming unemployed. They had taken many misdemeanors, or trivial offenses care of as felonies, with severe fines.[94]

The Pig Laws and regulations stayed in the books for many years and were expanded with a lot more discriminatory laws and regulations after the Jim Crow (state and local laws passed to re-enforce racial segregation in the southern states in the United States of America to keep oppressed) era began.
Free black groups existed up and down the eastern seaboard of North America. The largest is at Philadelphia, which with the impact of Quaker antislavery activists gained, opened its doors to black women and men within the middle of the eighteenth century. Some other cities with significant populations of free blacks were Boston, Providence, New York, and Charleston. The first man killed within the Boston Massacre of 1770 had been Crispus Attucks, a free mixed-race mariner. Four African Americans were in the Battle of Lexington in the American Revolution, plus some historians have estimated that around one-fifth of the rebel army that recaptured Boston from the British was black. Although George

---

[93] Black Codes and Pig Laws | Slavery By Another Name Bento | PBS.
https://www.pbs.org/tpt/slavery-by-another-name/themes/black-codes/
[94] Black Codes and Pig Laws | Slavery By Another Name Bento | PBS.
https://www.pbs.org/tpt/slavery-by-another-name/themes/black-codes/

Washington discouraged free men of color from enlisting in the Continental Army, they joined.[95]

Within the southern colonies through the Revolution, free blacks served in colonial regiments and militias but were more likely to help the British. At war's end, they transported all black loyalists to North America, Britain, the Western Indies, or Sierra Leone, condensing the South's already minor free black inhabitants. In 1790, the state with the principal inhabitants of free blacks was Virginia.[96]

The era of the First Republic within the U. S. saw the formal abolition of slavery in most northern states, along with the creation from Northwest Place, where they outlawed slavery from the beginning. Even on top of the South, the number of manumissions rose. The free African American population from the North grew to 27,000 in 1790 to 138,000 in 1830. In the South, it went from 30, 000 to 150, 000. This rise in population was due to natural growth. In states like Pennsylvania, Ohio, Maryland, and Indiana, fugitive slaves were a contributing factor. However, some new states of the Midwest, notably Illinois, enacted severe "Black Laws" to limit African American migration states like Maryland, Pennsylvania, Ohio, and Indiana, fugitive slaves, were a contributing factor. Many of the new states of the Midwest, notably Illinois, introduced extreme "Black Laws" to restrict the African American movement.[97]

Free individuals of color worked in a wide variety of professions. In the North, many bought little small farms. Land possession by free blacks within the South had been less frequent, and the ones who proved helpful in agriculture had been overseers and from time to time, bookkeepers, business managers, and attorneys over the farms of white relatives. Many white planters preferred to use free blacks as managers because they would

---

[95] "Free People of Color in Louisiana - LSU Libraries.
https://lib.lsu.edu/sites/all/files/sc/fpoc/history.html. Accessed 15 Aug. 2020.
[96] "Antebellum Period - HistoryNet. https://www.historynet.com/antebellum-period. Accessed 15 Aug. 2020.
[97] Free People of Color in Louisiana.
https://www.lib.lsu.edu/sites/all/files/sc/fpoc/history.html

work for a lower salary than whites and were more familiar with slave culture. Where the manager and worker were related-white fathers used their mixed-race children-there may have come a component of faith beyond what might have persisted had the employee been a slave or an unrelated                     white                     employee.[98]

Free people of color periodically became wealthy agriculturalists and businesspeople in their own right, in Louisiana. The navy and vendor marine were different various professional pathways for free black males. Some became artisans and artisans or labored as novice employees at opportunities that white individuals did not want to do. Many became ministers or, in Christian segments, including Louisiana, took religious orders. Free African American women in cities found work as domestic servants, washerwomen, and tailors—a fortunate few owned boarding houses.     The     least     fortunate     worked     as     prostitutes.[99]

The conditions in which free individuals of color lived varied, but were often deplorable, in northern cities, where several could just afford to lodge in attics and cellars. Though free, they still experienced racial prejudice. As historian Donald Wright offers written, " because many northern whites condemned slavery did not imply that they cared for persons of African descent. " Most saw blacks as substandard and as opponents                     for                     jobs.[100]

As part of both North to South, free African Americans encountered segregation in public areas. Mob physical violence directed at African American inhabitants happened in some northern metropolitan areas in the beginning 19th century. African American places of worship in N.Y. and Philadelphia vandalized, and in Providence in 1824, a white gang tore down every single building in one of the city's black communities. A riot

---

[98] "Antebellum Period - HistoryNet. https://www.historynet.com/antebellum-period. Accessed 15 Aug. 2020.
[99] "Free People of Color in Louisiana - LSU Libraries.
https://lib.lsu.edu/sites/all/files/sc/fpoc/history.html. Accessed 15 Aug. 2020.
[100] "Free People of Color in Louisiana - LSU Libraries.
https://lib.lsu.edu/sites/all/files/sc/fpoc/history.html. Accessed 15 Aug. 2020.

in Cincinnati in 1829 led to a lot over 1, 000 African Americans leading to America and going to Canada.[101]

They used the severe societal and settling circumstances of black females and males in Northern society an assertion in opposition to emancipation by slavery's defenders, who genuinely thought that free African Americans in northern cities were even worse off than slaves on southern plantations.[102]

Incongruously, given its later history, there is one place where free individuals of color enjoyed a higher level of acceptance and prosperity during the eighteenth hundred years: Louisiana. Though Virginia, Maryland, and Pennsylvania all had larger free black inhabitants, their impact and social significance were most considerable in Louisiana.[103]

The first free blacks in Louisiana were slaves who escaped and lived with American Indian tribes. A court case from 1722 is the 1st record of a free man of color in the attempting colony. 2 yrs. Later, a free black man went against a whitened man—the first record of a wedding between two free people of color schedules from 1725. Louis Congo, Louisiana's original executioner, was a free African American man. Another, Jean Congo, mentioned in the 1726 census as a toll collector and keeper of the High Road along with Bayou St. John, documenting that some individuals of color in colonial Louisiana held qualified positions.

In the wintertime of 1729-30, the Natchez Indians set a military blockade to Fort Rosalie at what is today Natchez, Mississippi. They presented countless slaves who fought against the French relief power and their independence in incentive for their service. [104] The first persisting

[101] "Free People of Color in Louisiana - LSU Libraries. https://lib.lsu.edu/sites/all/files/sc/fpoc/history.html. Accessed 15 Aug. 2020.
[102] "Free People of Color in Louisiana - LSU Libraries. https://lib.lsu.edu/sites/all/files/sc/fpoc/history.html. Accessed 15 Aug. 2020.
[103] "Free Blacks in the Antebellum Period - The African American .... https://www.loc.gov/exhibits/african-american-odyssey/free-blacks-in-the-antebellum-period.html. Accessed 15 Aug. 2020.
[104]

evidence of a slave manumission dates from 1733, when Jean-Baptiste Le Moyne, Sieur de Bienville, New Orleans's originator, freed two slaves who were in their service for twenty-six years.[105] It became a mutual practice in Louisiana for elderly slaves to be freed and, besides masters, within their wills, to free individual slaves or entire families.[106]

In 1763, France conceded Louisiana to Spain to cover it due to its closings inside the 7 Years' War. The colony's transfer marked the start of the absolute best period that is liberal Louisiana's history about free individuals of color. The Spanish enacted a set that is new called Las Siete Partidas. These guidelines offered slaves more protection that is excellent mistreatment by whites making it more accessible for them to buy their freedom.

African Americans who had been already free could now provide into the militia, buy, and offer their slaves, and they protected them from arbitrary authorities' queries. Although legislation forbidding mixed-race marriages, it turned out ignored. Free individuals of color could live everyday lives, not remarkably distinctive from those of whites of comparable social and status that is economical.[107]

Furthermore, marriages, extramarital relationships involving the events existed. It became an acknowledged practice in Louisiana for white men (wedded and unmarried) to consider black paramours. These interactions were longstanding. Some historians have contended that free women of color desired to function as mistresses of whitened men since it better their status and security and their children's. Dozens of these females in the late eighteenth century bought valuable houses through their interactions with their whitened companions or fathers.

By one estimation, a quarter of the houses along the main streets of New

---

105

[106] "Free Blacks in the Antebellum Period - The African American ....
https://www.loc.gov/exhibits/african-american-odyssey/free-blacks-in-the-antebellum-period.html. Accessed 15 Aug. 2020.
[107] "Free People of Color in Louisiana - LSU Libraries.
https://lib.lsu.edu/sites/all/files/sc/fpoc/history.html. Accessed 15 Aug. 2020.

Orleans owned by free African Americans, many of whom were single ladies. At Natchitoches in the central area of Louisiana, Marie Thérèse Metoyer (better known as "Coincoin") handled various large estates directed at her through a French public with whom she gained a 25 years-long liaison and ten kids. (Her offspring produced the foundation of the considerable negotiation of free people of color that lived along the Cane River.) Successions of prominent whitened men as past due as the 1850s acknowledge and bequeath house or money to their illegitimate children of color.

Historians have argued that, in some other instances, it was the woman who had the top economic hand in like arrangements once the whitened man enjoyed less financial shows than she.[108]

Throughout the Louisiana purchase in 1803, a minimum of one in six for the approximately 8, 000 individuals living in New Orleans was a free individual of color. The town's populace, both black and white, over doubled between 1791 and 1810 because of an influx of émigrés displaced from the Haitian Trend (directed by Toussaint Louverture, a free man of color). The initial formal U. S. census of Orleans Place in 1810 totaled 7, 585 free individuals of color, equated to 34, 311 whites and a total populace of 76, 556.[109]

The influx of black colored refugees from Haiti heightened anxieties among Louisiana's white populace. The colony/ territory had only barely escaped several slave rebellions over the previous twenty years. Free individuals of color, some argue, would incite unrest that is further—the problem compounded with all the departure in 1803 through the Spanish.

Territorial governor William C. C. Claiborne was forced not just by leader Thomas Jefferson's management but by Louisiana's French-speaking inhabitants that are white lessen the number of free males of color who

[108] "Slavery in the Colonies | Boundless US History.
https://courses.lumenlearning.com/boundless-ushistory/chapter/slavery-in-the-colonies/. Accessed 15 Aug. 2020.
[109] "The Domestic Slave Trade - AAME :.
http://www.inmotionaame.org/print.cfm?migration=3. Accessed 15 Aug. 2020.

served in the militia. Some wished to see a decrease in how big the free black                                    population                            was.[110]

In 1806, the territorial legislature flushed an act (in no way fully enforced) prohibiting free black adult males from entering Louisiana and ordering those older than fifteen whom they blessed elsewhere to depart (Louisiana's indigenous free individuals of color were given U. S. citizenship in 1803). In 1812, 12 months following the German that failed (the most massive slave rebellion in U. S. history), the government denied free black males the right to vote.[111]

Throughout this era and before the abolition of slavery produced their legal split status, free people of color had been necessary to carry passes, observe curfews, and to possess their racial standing designated in every public record.[112]

Golden Age: The Early Antebellum Era, 1812-1830

Whatever the limitations imposed through the territorial period, the giving of statehood in 1812 coincided with the start of the "golden age" of free people of color in Louisiana. The Caribbean, or Latin America, others remained behind, lured by Louisiana's booming economy (at the outbreak of the Civil War through several for European countries, the state has been the richest within the Union and New Orleans the 3rd most significant town).

Free women of color and men could very own, inherit, and market property, which includes slaves. Vast plantations in the outskirts of New Orleans had been marketed off and subdivided to create brand-new neighborhoods where free blacks bought plots of land alongside whites. Many became involved in prestigious New Orleans interpersonal and

---

[110] "Slavery in the United States - EH.net. https://eh.net/encyclopedia/slavery-in-the-united-states/. Accessed 15 Aug. 2020.
[111] Free People of Color in Louisiana.
https://www.lib.lsu.edu/sites/all/files/sc/fpoc/history.html
[112] "History of slavery in Maryland -. https://en.
/History of slavery in Maryland. Accessed 15 Aug. 2020.

cultural institutions such as opera, theaters, balls, benevolent groups, and the church. Louisiana's free black population rose from slightly below 11,000 in 1820 to about 25,000 in 1840, maintaining pace using the increase of whitened and slave populations and representing about seven percent from the state's total people.[113]

Free individuals of color worked in lots of trades that white people worked inside, which range from shop keeping and common unskilled labor to even more specific lines of work such as carpentry, stone cutting, and metalworking.

Historian David Rankin noted from the 1850 census that of all American towns, New Orleans " experienced the highest portion of free black men used as artisans, professionals, and entrepreneurs, and the cheapest in 'low possibility' professions like laborer, mariner, gardener, servant, and waiter. New Orleans had more significant than a quarter of most free men of color used as professionals, managers, artists, clerks, and scientists within the fifteen most significant cities in America.[114]

It concerns efforts to the creative arts that Louisiana's free individuals of color became most known. Many distinguished themselves as writers. Armand Lanusse printed Les Cenelles, an anthology of poetry by free males of color, in 1845. One factor to work, Victor Séjour, is Louisiana's best playwright that is the French language. Jules Lion, one of Louisiana's very first lithographers, had been indigenous of France who founded New Orleans around 1830; he considered to have introduced photography to the state. Eugène and Daniel Warburg, sons of the German-Jewish estate that is real and their servant, became respected sculptors and marble employees, carving most of the elaborate tombs, which is why New Orleans is distinguished.[115]

---

[113] "History of slavery in Maryland -. https://en.org/i/History_of_slavery_in_Maryland. Accessed 15 Aug. 2020.
[114] "Slavery in the United States - EH.net. https://eh.net/encyclopedia/slavery-in-the-united-states/. Accessed 15 Aug. 2020.
[115] "Free People of Color in Louisiana - LSU Libraries. https://lib.lsu.edu/sites/all/files/sc/fpoc/history.html. Accessed 15 Aug. 2020.

A few free individuals of color were highly prosperous running a business. The vendor and property agent Bernard Soulié doubled his capital from $50, 000 to $100, 000 within the 1850s. Ten years early in the day, Eulalie de Mandeville Macarty gained her fortune of $150, 000 via a mixture of presents from the lover that is white, her family members' wide range, and her very own dry products company. Pierre Casanave, the Haitian-born clerk of the businessperson that is Jewish philanthropist Judah Touro, used the $10, 000 legacy that their boss left him setting himself up as a payment vendor and undertaker. By 1864, he had been well worth $100, 000.

Thomy Lafon accumulated the most fortunate that is considerable of a million dollars-through brokering and home conjecture and ended up being among Louisiana's many prominent philanthropists, adding to charities, schools, hospitals, and antislavery communities. Another philanthropist, Marie Couvent, the African-born widow for the wealthy businessman that is black Couvent, kept profit when she died in 1837 used to find the Institute Catholique, among the first schools in America to educate children of African descent.

The child of just one for the earliest descendants of free people of color in New Orleans, Henriette Delille, produced a title for herself because the creator for the Sisters for the Holy Family, the 2nd earliest Catholic order that is religious ladies of color. The Sisters caused poor people, the ill, older people, and among slaves, founded a college for females in 1850, and exposed a medical center for needy Orleanians that are black.[116]

Louis Charles Roudanez, trained to be a physician in France and New England, owned an active practice that is medical New Orleans within the 1850s, dealing with both light and black patients. In 1864, he started posting the French-language La Tribune de la Nouvelle Orléans, the country's first African American daily newspaper. Norbert Rillieux, though not a businessman, contributed significantly to the business life of Louisiana when he invented, in 1843, a new manner of sugar refining that

[116] "The "Nous" of Southern Catholic Quadroons: Racial, Ethnic ....
https://www.researchgate.net/publication/31018177 The Nous of Southern Catholic Quadroons Racial Ethnic and Religious Identity in Les Cenelles. Accessed 15 Aug. 2020.

revolutionized                     the                     settlement.[117]

Lately, historians have checked beyond New Orleans at free black populations in other areas of Louisiana, where they were just as productive. The first report of a free black living within the prairies of southwestern Louisiana is from 1766. The 1774 census of the Opelousas area shows that this same man owned two slaves and fifty cattle, a noteworthy fact when, according to historian Carl Brasseaux, just 22% of families in this section of Louisiana owned slaves and only 18 percent of freeholders possessed fifty cattle.[118] In 1810, white males in the community around Opelousas outnumbered white females by a margin of 500, leading to liaisons with slaves that grew into common-law marriages where       they       emancipated       the       female.[119]

Matriarchs influenced many free black families. Marie Simien, in 1818, had nine servants and added more than seventy-five hundred acres of real property, including 1, 400 acres of leading cultivated land in St. Landry Parish. The biggest category concerning free black planters and vendors outside of New Orleans was the Metoyer family members of Natchitoches Parish, who intermarried with other black planters. In 1830, the family-owned eight percent of the servants in Natchitoches Parish.

Many individuals had no property or slaves but performed as plantation overseers. Aaron Griggs, for instance, worked on Antonio Patrick Walsh's plantation in West Feliciana Parish in the 1820s. Others stayed in communities, typically working as building contractors.

Free African Americans were living in Baton Rouge, at minimum, as early as 1782. In 1850, eighty of the 159 free African Americans in Lafayette Parish were living in Vermilionville (now Lafayette), and half of the free

---

[117] "Haitian Immigration to Louisiana in the Eighteenth ... - AAME :.
http://www.inmotionaame.org/texts/viewer.cfm?id=5_000T. Accessed 15 Aug. 2020.
[118]Free People of Color in Louisiana.
https://www.lib.lsu.edu/sites/all/files/sc/fpoc/history.html
[119] "Les Cenelles: Choix de poésies indigènes · DSCF.
http://silverbox.gmu.edu/dscff/s/aaaw/item/476. Accessed 15 Aug. 2020.

black populace of St. Martin Parish was living in the communities of St. Martinsville and New Iberia. Many free black people of the "bayou land" escaped in the 1850s as racial trepidation mounted, and they drove many of those who continued out in 1859 by groups of Caucasian vigilantes.[120]

Many southerners, already within the defensive regarding slavery, worried that free people of color would collaborate with abolitionists. With southerners' perceived danger to slavery, race-based distinctions became more important than one's lawful status. Both slave and free because of this, Louisiana's " fantastic age group " of free people of color fell into weakening around 1830, the starting of an era of harsh legislation about African Americans.[121] It became a criminal activity to create anything criticizing supremacy that is white masters wanting to free their slaves had to create a $1, 000 bond guaranteeing that freed slaves would leave Hawaii within four weeks, and whites prohibited all blacks from testifying against whites in court.[122]

In 1855, they prohibited free people of color from assembling or developing any organizations that are new communities.[123] The emancipation of slaves ended up being outlawed totally in 1857, and, as through the territorial period, free persons of color had to carry passes to move from one place to another in a specific location, observe curfews, and have their racial status designated in every public record.[124]

Other factors furthermore played a component in free blacks leaving behind Louisiana. An influx of Irish and immigrants that are German who displaced free black merchants and were ready to work on unskilled

[120] "Les Cenelles: Choix de poésies indigènes · DSCF. http://silverbox.gmu.edu/dscff/s/aaaw/item/476. Accessed 15 Aug. 2020.
[121] Free People of Color in Louisiana. https://www.lib.lsu.edu/sites/all/files/sc/fpoc/history.html
[122] Free People of Color in Louisiana. https://www.lib.lsu.edu/sites/all/files/sc/fpoc/history.html
[123] Free People of Color in Louisiana. https://www.lib.lsu.edu/sites/all/files/sc/fpoc/history.html
[124] "Haitian Immigration : Eighteenth and Nineteenth ... - AAME :. http://www.inmotionaame.org/print.cfm?migration=5. Accessed 15 Aug. 2020.

careers for low earnings started in the 1830s. The strain of 1837 affected their state and pressured some blacks that were wealthy to offer the home because of many elements, Louisiana's free inhabitants black in the following 20 years. Many kept finding a much better life within the North, France, Haiti, and Latin America. Some, without doubt, they could "pass" as white, so no more had been counted among free individuals of color. Other people relocated to Africa and Mexico by colonization communities. A reduction from 7. 7 percent in 1830 on the eve for the Civil War, free individuals of color represented just 2. 6 percent for the populace                     of                     Louisiana.[125]

People who stayed faced divided loyalties once the Civil War broke away in 1861. In May of that 12 months, about 1, 500 free black New Orleanians responded to Confederate governor Thomas Overton Moore's demand for troops, developing the Louisiana Local Safeguard. Although its colonel had been white, it had been the first military service device in American history to have black officers. In the Cane River area of northwest Louisiana, two free units that are black created, the Augustin Guards and Monette's Guards. Why free people of color volunteered to guard the Confederacy is a matter of debate. Some may have seen it to enhance their position in society. Others feared the harm that they or their property if they did not conform. Following the fall of New Orleans, some Native Guard members formed a new unit within the Union Army. Swelled by runaway slaves, they split into three regiments, two which took part in the siege of Port Hudson. Captain André Cailloux, a respected businessperson before the war, was killed in action. Their death, reported within the press, became a rallying cry for African United states recruitment.[126]

For free individuals of color who owned plantations and slaves, the war was a blended blessing, bringing better freedom, but destroying the state's

---

[125] Free People of Color in Louisiana.
https://www.lib.lsu.edu/sites/all/files/sc/fpoc/history.html
[126] "Haitian Immigration to Louisiana in the Eighteenth ... - AAME :.
http://www.inmotionaame.org/texts/viewer.cfm?id=5_000T. Accessed 15 Aug. 2020.

economy and causing significant property loss.[127] A string of droughts and crop failures, alongside them, must grow food instead of cash crops through the Union blockade, contributing towards the economic turmoil. Whites did not spare the plantations owned by free people of color from the ravages of Union troops, who carried down livestock, plants, farm implements, and home products.[128] Without capital, slaves, or money to employ workers, free black planters had to work their very own fields.[129]

As historian Gary Mills has written, " Rather than elevation to a posture of full citizenship and equality, the once-influential groups of color were now publicly submerged into the new mass of black freedmen-a class and culture with that they had no identification and something that harbored much resentment toward them. "[130]

Legacies: Louisiana's "Creoles of Color" following the Civil War

Although all African American planters, like their white counterparts, abandoned from the Civil War, added free individuals of color prospered within the war's wake. In politics, they appeared because of the frontrunners for Louisiana's black human population. The child of a white Georgian planter and his slave became one of Louisiana's administrators; they later elected him to Congress during Reconstruction, they elected many to the state legislature, and for an abbreviated time, P. B. S. Pinchback.

Despite their typical situation that is political, however, English-speaking African Americans, such as Pinchback, were not accepted as leaders using a Creole elite that has their unique aspirations to leadership. These two camps crystallized around two newspapers, one started by Pinchback

---

[127] Free People of Color in Louisiana.
https://www.lib.lsu.edu/sites/all/files/sc/fpoc/history.html
[128] Free People of Color in Louisiana.
https://www.lib.lsu.edu/sites/all/files/sc/fpoc/history.html
[129] Free People of Color in Louisiana.
https://www.lib.lsu.edu/sites/all/files/sc/fpoc/history.html
[130] "Haitian Immigration : Eighteenth and Nineteenth ... - AAME :.
http://www.inmotionaame.org/print.cfm?migration=5. Accessed 15 Aug. 2020.

and one by the prominent physician Charles Roudanez. The latter's La Tribune de la Nouvelle Orléans / The New Orleans Tribune was a French-English newspaper printed from 1864 to 1870. The first black daily paper in the United States, it came to assist as the voice of the Creoles of Color (a term implemented after the Civil War but still used today to appoint people descended from free individuals of color). Pinchback's Louisianan, in its various forms, enjoyed an extended run from 1870 to 1882 and was found with English-speaking blacks.[131]

Such ethnicity-based distinctions lessened in the face of Jim Crow laws of the late nineteenth century. Because of these discriminatory regulations, black political influence waned. However, even then, the descendants of free people of color, who could keep in mind the so-called " fantastic age" of the first nineteenth century, continued to challenge racial prejudices and segregation laws. The most well-known case was that of Homer Plessy, who tried to ride a New Orleans streetcar for whites only. The Comité des Citoyens, which composed primarily of French speaking-free individuals of color, organized a legal suit on the incident that had become referred to as the landmark case Plessy v. Ferguson. The efforts backfired, however, once the U. S. The Supreme Court upheld the constitutionality of the "separate but equal" doctrine, a notice would stick until 1954.

Creoles of Color persisted in collaborating with other African Americans to contest injustice and encourage progressive whites to sustain black institutions, such as Xavier and Dillard Universities and the Flint-Goodridge Hospital and Nursing School.[132] In the twentieth century, attorney A. P. Tureaud sued that led to the end of school separation in New Orleans.[133] His son, A. P. Tureaud, Jr. turned out to be the first black student to register at Louisiana State University in Baton Rouge. Additional progeny of free people of color, Ernest N. "Dutch" Morial,

---

[131] "Les Cenelles: Choix de poésies indigènes · DSCF. http://silverbox.gmu.edu/dscff/s/aaaw/item/476. Accessed 15 Aug. 2020.
[132] Free People of Color in Louisiana. https://www.lib.lsu.edu/sites/all/files/sc/fpoc/history.html
[133] Free People of Color in Louisiana. https://www.lib.lsu.edu/sites/all/files/sc/fpoc/history.html

became    New    Orleans's    first    black    mayor    in    1977.[134]

Some can trace the legacy of Louisiana's free people of color in what may be the state's most significant contribution to world-jazz.[135] Merging European and African musical traditions, men such as Alphonse Picou, Jimmy Palao, Manuel Perez, Freddie Keppard, Ferdinand Joseph LaMothe (better known as Jelly Roll Morton), and subsequently, Sidney Bechet produced a unique sound that became associated with Louisiana and inspired many instrumentalists of all backgrounds. This quintessentially American craft form, which for over a millennium has welcomed not only assorted individuals but various strategies, is a suitable memorial to free men and women of color.[136] In jazz, as the late Dave Brubeck stated, "Kinship does not come from pores and skin. It is in the soul and the mind."[137]

[134] "Les Cenelles: Choix de poésies indigènes · DSCF.
http://silverbox.gmu.edu/dscff/s/aaaw/item/476. Accessed 15 Aug. 2020.
[135] Free People of Color in Louisiana.
https://www.lib.lsu.edu/sites/all/files/sc/fpoc/history.html
[136] Free People of Color in Louisiana.
https://www.lib.lsu.edu/sites/all/files/sc/fpoc/history.html
[137] "Les Cenelles: Choix de poésies indigènes · DSCF.
http://silverbox.gmu.edu/dscff/s/aaaw/item/476. Accessed 15 Aug. 2020.

# Chapter 4 Louisiana Voodoo

Louisiana Voodoo (French: Vaudou Louisiana), recognized as New Orleans Voodoo, describes a set of religious beliefs and practices put together from the customs of the African dispersion in Louisiana.[138] They sometimes refer to it as Mississippi Valley Voodoo whenever referring to its historical reputation and development in the more significant Mississippi Valley. It is a social development of the Afro-American religious beliefs came into being by the West and Central African populations of the U.S. state of Louisiana. Voodoo is one of the countless incarnations of African-structured spiritual folkways, rooted in West African Dahomeyan Vodun.[139]

Voodoo's liturgical language is Louisiana Creole, one of the two principal heritage languages (the remaining becoming Louisiana French) of the Louisiana Creole people. It turned into syncretized with the Catholic and Francophone culture of New Orleans because of the African cultural oppressiveness in the region as part of the Atlantic slave trade. Louisiana Voodoo is often perplexed with Haitian Vodou and Deep Southern Hoodoo, but, although associated with these kinds of religious beliefs, is a belief structure of its own. It fluctuates from Haitian Vodou in its emphasis on gris-gris, Voodoo queens, use of Hoodoo paraphernalia, and Li Grand Zombi. It was through Louisiana Voodoo that such words as gris-gris (a Wolof term) and "Voodoo dolls'" was presented into the American lexicon.[140]

## Gris-Gris

---

[138] "Voodoo Religions: Beliefs & Rituals - Video & Lesson ....
https://study.com/academy/lesson/voodoo-religions-beliefs-rituals.html.
Accessed 15 Aug. 2020.
[139] "Voodoo Religions: Beliefs & Rituals - Video & Lesson ....
https://study.com/academy/lesson/voodoo-religions-beliefs-rituals.html.
Accessed 15 Aug. 2020.
[140] "A trinity of beliefs and a unity of the sacred: modern Vodou ....
https://pdfs.semanticscholar.org/89f6/c17f361d0b62146ba4668578bf63b1007d09.pdf. Accessed 15 Aug. 2020.

Gris-gris is a Voodoo amulet beginning in Africa, which guarded the wearer against evilness or luck that brings plus in some West African nations a method of birth control. It has a small cloth, inscribed with verses from an African ancestor having a ritual number of small objects, used on the person.[141]

## Etymology of Gris-Gris

While the exact background of the word is mysterious, some historians trace the word back to the Yoruba word juju, meaning fetish. An alternate theory is that the word originates aided by the French joujou, meaning doll or plaything. They attributed scholarly sources to the Mandingo word meaning "MAGIC.[142]

---

[141] "The Voodoo Hoodoo Spellbook - MetaphysicSpirit.com. http://www.metaphysicspirit.com/books/The%20Voodoo%20Hoodoo%20Spellbook.pdf. Accessed 15 Aug. 2020.

[142] "The Voodoo Hoodoo Spellbook - MetaphysicSpirit.com. http://www.metaphysicspirit.com/books/The%20Voodoo%20Hoodoo%20Spellbook.pdf. Accessed 15 Aug. 2020.

## History of Gris-Gris

The gris-gris began in Dagomba in Ghana and is associated with Islamic traditions. In the beginning, the gris-gris had been adorned with Islamic scripture and used to ward off evil spirits (evil djinn) or poor fortune. Historians of the right time noted that non-believers and believers wore them likewise and found them attached to buildings.[143]

The practice of using gris-gris, though originating in Africa, came to the United States with enslaved Africans and was adopted by professionals of Voodoo. The practice soon changed, and the gris-gris created black magic upon their "victim. Slaves would often use the gris-gris against their owners, plus some observed adorning their tombs. During this period, individuals reported slaves cutting, drowning, or manipulating the gris-gris of others to cause harm. Although in Haiti, gris-gris is an amulet suitable for an element of a practiced religion; in the Cajun communities of Louisiana, gris-gris was a symbol of black magic and ill-fortune.

Despite the negative connotations of gris-gris, so-called Gris-Gris medical practitioners have worked in the Creole communities of Louisiana for some centuries and are looked at favorably by the community. In the 1800s, gris-gris was implemented interchangeably in Louisiana to mean both bewitch and about the traditional amulet. Some used Gris-gris in Neo-Hoodoo, which has its origins in Voodoo. In this context, a gris-gris expresses the self. Rootwork was known as Hoodoo.[144]

Somewhere around 388,000 African people from various ethnic teams had been delivered to North America (including Canada) involving the seventeenth and nineteenth hundreds of years because of the transatlantic slave trade. They had been Malagasy, Kongo, Igbo, Maghrebis (Moors), Akhan, Mandé, Hausa, and Fulbe, among many others. Hoodoo started shortly after Indigenous People in the United States, enslaved Africans,

---

[143] "The Voodoo Hoodoo Spellbook - MetaphysicSpirit.com. http://www.metaphysicspirit.com/books/The%20Voodoo%20Hoodoo%20Spellbook.pdf. Accessed 15 Aug. 2020.
[144] "The Voodoo Hoodoo Spellbook - MetaphysicSpirit.com. http://www.metaphysicspirit.com/books/The%20Voodoo%20Hoodoo%20Spellbook.pdf. Accessed 15 Aug. 2020.

and Europeans came into the day-to-day experience of one another through the colonial era. [145]

The many accepted narrative categorizes Hoodoo as being retention that is primarily African Native American and European influences. Scholars can classify several aspects of rootwork that as African retention (such as bone tissue divination, quartered ideographic, religious symbols, medication bundles,.) are ubiquitous to many native American countries too.[146]

The level to which Hoodoo could be practiced diverse by area plus the temperament associated with servant owners. Enslaved Africans for the Southeast, referred to as Gullah, experienced isolation and freedom that is allowed for retention associated with the methods of these West African ancestors.

Zora Neal Hurston, an African American social anthropologist and Hoodoo report inside her essay Hoodoo in America, that Hoodoo or conjure, had its most significant development across the Gulf Coast, into the municipality of New Orleans and the surrounding nation. It had been those areas Haitian immigrants settled that after the overthrow of this French guideline in Haiti by Toussaint Louverture.[147]

1000s of mulattoes and Haitians of African descent, along with their white ex-masters, had been driven away, the nearest refuge that is French the province of Louisiana. They brought using them their conjure rituals changed by connection with European tradition, including the Catholic church. Unlike the North American slaves, who traded like livestock or virtually any commodity with no thought fond of family members ties, island slaves were motivated to create by themselves the most significant

[145] "The Voodoo Hoodoo Spellbook - MetaphysicSpirit.com. http://www.metaphysicspirit.com/books/The%20Voodoo%20Hoodoo%20Spellbook.pdf. Accessed 15 Aug. 2020.
[146] "The Voodoo Hoodoo Spellbook - MetaphysicSpirit.com. http://www.metaphysicspirit.com/books/The%20Voodoo%20Hoodoo%20Spellbook.pdf. Accessed 15 Aug. 2020.
[147] "African amulets. http://dpositive.com.ng/enb/african-amulets.html. Accessed 15 Aug. 2020.

amount of at-home as one can in their bondage. They thus kept more of the West African background, customs, and language compared to the continental slaves.[148]

Thirteen hundred transports from Haiti settled in Louisiana from 1791 to 1809, bringing an infusion string of French West Africa techniques. Rootwork or Hoodoo, in the Mississippi Delta in which the concentration of enslaved African Americans was thick, they practiced under a large cover. They distributed Hoodoo throughout the entire United States as African Americans left the delta through the Great Migration.

Hoodoo was first documented in American English in 1875 and had to be a noun (the training of Hoodoo) or as being a transitive verb, since in "we hoodoo the person," an action performed by varying means. The Hoodoo could be manifest in a recovery potion, or into the exercise of the parapsychological energy, or as the cause of damage which befalls the targeted victim.[149]

In African American Vernacular English (AAVE), Hoodoo is used to refer to a paranormal consciousness or spiritual hypnotherapy, a spell, but Hoodoo may be an adjective for the practitioner, such as in "Hoodoo man. Known Hoodoo spells date straight back towards the 1800s. Spells are reliant about the intention associated with the practitioner and "reading" for the customer.[150]

---

[148] "The Encyclopedia of Witches, Witchcraft and Wicca - Semantic .... 1 Mar. 2020, https://pdfs.semanticscholar.org/5873/43e3cc13020a3e417282e159c2c79db2 19ed.pdf. Accessed 15 Aug. 2020.
[149] "The Encyclopedia of Witches, Witchcraft and Wicca - Semantic .... 1 Mar. 2020, https://pdfs.semanticscholar.org/5873/43e3cc13020a3e417282e159c2c79db2 19ed.pdf. Accessed 15 Aug. 2020.
[150] "The Encyclopedia of Witches, Witchcraft and Wicca - Semantic .... 1 Mar. 2020, https://pdfs.semanticscholar.org/5873/43e3cc13020a3e417282e159c2c79db2 19ed.pdf. Accessed 15 Aug. 2020.

Marie Catherine Laveau

# Chapter 5 The True History and Faith Behind Voodoo

The Voodoo Experience, with its taglines "join the ritual," and "ritual the music," pegs its calendar to Halloween season. It has become a tradition in New Orleans, often like All Saints' Day, when families head to the cemeteries associated with French Quarter and beyond to whitewash and clean the tombs neat and decorate all of them with fresh plants.[151]

Jerry Gandolfo, a native New Orleanian whose family has run the Voodoo Museum into the French Quarter in the 1970s, features seen oodles of products and locations that take the title voodoo. One used the word in terms like voodoo economics and voodoo science. In a festival kept out-of-doors, beneath the live oaks, the drums and music could invite the spirits and echo the last, living up to its title Voodoo. "If done right, the music should take ownership of the person. One would not stand. If that takes place, one is doing Voodoo," he suggested. "There is continuity.[152]

## Voodoo's New Orleans Roots

Voodoo appeared in New Orleans during the early 1700s, through slaves brought from Africa's western "slave coast. Like plenty of things in New Orleans, Voodoo was then infused using the town's prominent religion, Catholicism, and became a Voodoo-Catholicism hybrid, often referred to as New Orleans Voodoo. In New Orleans, for instance, Legba, the Voodoo deity who controls the gates towards the character world, becomes St. Peter, just who keeps the secrets to the gates of paradise.[153]

---

[151] "The True History and Faith Behind Voodoo - French Quarter. https://www.frenchquarter.com/true-history-faith-behind-voodoo/. Accessed 15 Aug. 2020.

[152] "The True History and Faith Behind Voodoo - French Quarter. https://www.frenchquarter.com/true-history-faith-behind-voodoo/. Accessed 15 Aug. 2020.

[153] "French Quarter History | Walking History Tours | Katrina and .... https://www.frenchquarter.com/history/2/. Accessed 15 Aug. 2020.

Marie Laveau, a devout catholic, went to Mass at St. Louis Cathedral and was a friend associated with the cathedral's priest, Pere Antoine.

These days, Voodoo lives on in New Orleans through individuals who notice it as an element of their tradition, through error-prone rumor, and the long shadow of Laveau, the city's best-known Voodoo.

In-front of Laveau's brick-and-mortar tomb in St. Louis # 1 cemetery about the borders of the French Quarter, fans layaway stacks of nickels, paper flowers, and other choices. Seeing cemeteries like this one is one of the more popular things one can do within the quarter French beyond.[154]

## Marie Laveau Tomb French Quarter

Whenever Laveau was living and living on St. Ann Street, men and women made use of knocking on her behalf at all hours, looking for help, meals, or guidance about a straying husband. Her death in 1881 did not stop that. "In Voodoo, an ancestor can be much alive as a living person.

Laveau, who was known as the Widow Paris after the death of her first spouse Jacques Paris, was a striking figure that is spiritual, a do-gooder, and a no-cost girl of shade. She followed orphans, fed the hungry, visited prisoners, and nursed countless patients back to wellness during the yellow-fever epidemic.[155] She had been a naturopath skilled at treating customers with therapeutic massage, teas, natural herbs, salves, and tinctures, which had been more successful with yellow-fever parents than bloodletting and other

---

[154] "From Marie Laveau to Voodoo Festival in New Orleans. 5 Apr. 2019, http://laventurelouisianaise.blogspot.com/2019/04/from-marie-laveau-to-voodoo-festival-in.html. Accessed 15 Aug. 2020.
[155] The True History and Faith Behind Voodoo. https://www.frenchquarter.com/true-history-faith-behind-voodoo/

health practices associated with the time. Several publications cite first-hand reports of next-door neighbors remembering exactly how Laveau had flowers, candles, pictures of saints, and altars throughout her home, the way the front steps were scrubbed each morning with brick dust, to defend the house, and just how she experienced a statue of St Anthony of Padua, the patron saint of discovery lost products.[156]

## Today Voodoo in New Orleans

Hoodoo is a non-religious belief, the objects of Voodoo, or gris-gris. Gandolfo likens it to a belief that the four-leaf clover is happy. New Orleans has had a long-line of accessible hoodoo professionals and stores, and people right here talk about spells that use pictures of saints, chicken feet, graveyard dirt, brick-dust, gunpowder, pins and needles, candle lights and incense.[157]

---

[156] "From Marie Laveau to Voodoo Festival in New Orleans. 5 Apr. 2019, http://laventurelouisianaise.blogspot.com/2019/04/from-marie-laveau-to-voodoo-festival-in.html. Accessed 15 Aug. 2020.

[157] "The Voodoo Queen, the Cheerleader, and the ... - Nouvelle. https://c.nouvelle-ug.ru/26. Accessed 15 Aug. 2020.

# Chapter 6 From Benin to Bourbon Street: a history that is brief of Voodoo

The specter of Voodoo hangs heavily on the Crescent City, its presence felt from within garish traveler traps, and fading antebellum drawing rooms into the tiny burning altars kept hidden from spying eyes.[158] Much like the sprawling, confounding, bewitching town it calls residence, New Orleans voodoo itself is a distinctive and very porous entity, contains a variety of various values and enhanced by the severe hardships a lot of its initial practitioners. It is because of this strain that voodoo dolls, voodoo queens, and gris-gris first entered the U.S. lexicon and its pop culture, and it stays a giant social destination in New Orleans— though nowadays, companies make voodoo dolls in China.[159] Hell, the town has got a football team named for this. Voodoo is about since conventional as it gets in NOLA, that is all the stranger offered its convoluted and bloody history.[160]

The belief that is spiritual Voodoo originated from Africa, produced and associated with the West African conventional religion known as Voodoo or Vodou. Followers have confidence in the existence of one supreme god, attended by various spirits (loa), often manifested by the elements and every of who has its preferred sign (shade, good fresh fruit, number) and sacred element. The animal sacrifice of goats and birds is typical in some traditions, done by elders to harness the power of the spirit globe. Thanks to the Catholic impact, some loa later became synonymous with saints. They invoke ancestors for their knowledge and protection, and Louisiana voodoo

---

[158] From Benin to Bourbon Street: A Brief History of Louisiana ....
https://www.vice.com/en_us/article/r7g5ar/from-benin-to-bourbon-street-a-brief-history-of-louisiana-voodoo

[159] From Benin to Bourbon Street: A Brief History of Louisiana ....
https://www.vice.com/en_us/article/r7g5ar/from-benin-to-bourbon-street-a-brief-history-of-louisiana-voodoo

[160] "The True History and Faith Behind Voodoo - French Quarter.
https://www.frenchquarter.com/true-history-faith-behind-voodoo/. Accessed 15 Aug. 2020.

seems to have been a matriarchal being, with voodoo queens and priestesses holding power that is absolute. The faith has its roots in coastal West Africa from Ghana to Nigeria, but it is common when one looks at the Republic of Benin. A majority of Beninese take part in the Fon culture, and a linguistic group and "vodoun" is the Fon term for "spirits" or "gods. Through the transatlantic slave-trade, Benin discovered itself close to the epicenter about the Slave Coast, and a considerable part of newly arrived slaves that set foot into the French colony of Louisiana was of Fon origin. The roots of Voodoo included all of them.[161]

These captives introduced their particular languages, treating methods, and religious beliefs (like the ancestor worship and elder veneration that figure prominently in modern-day Voodoo) with them, and because French slave owners often held families collectively, these customs they maintained up to a great extent. The settlement was still in its beginning, with rigid colonial laws still developing now. The ratio of African to European colonizers hovered around two to one, and New Orleans society allowed gens de couleur libres (free people of shade), some of whom continued to become Voodoo's most significant numbers. Throughout this period, African culture—and spirituality—thrived in French Louisiana and became a fundamental element of the multicultural framework upon which they had built New Orleans. The United States banned the importation of overseas slaves in 1808. Louisiana's African community was already firmly set up; roots firmly planted in the spongy soil by the time. Voodoo had grown as a vital religious force, including new practices just like the Le Grand Zombi serpent and the using of amulets or small appeal bags known as gris-gris that should heal, aid, or harm (the sale of which aided

---

[161] "The True History and Faith Behind Voodoo - French Quarter. https://www.frenchquarter.com/true-history-faith-behind-voodoo/. Accessed 15 Aug. 2020.

many early voodoo queens to turn a severe tidy revenue).[162]

## Le Grand Zombi Serpent

Li Grand Zombi (referred to as Damballah Wedo) is the serpent major in worship among New Orleans Voodooists. In New Orleans Voodoo, they do not regard snakes as signs of bad as in the tale of Adam and Eve. Individuals thought that Snakes were the holders of intuitive knowledge. Women dance with serpents to portray the spiritual stability between the genders. Voodoo traditions in New Orleans always come with a snake dance to celebrate the web link into the old understanding. The foundation of Li Grand Zombi may derive the serpent deity Nzambi from Whydah in Africa.[163] According to the Bantu Creation story, Nzambi is the Creator God:

Nzambi is present in every little thing and controls the world through his appointed Spirits. In the beginning, only Nzambi existed. He counterclockwise until Ngombe was born, when he was ready to create millions and millions of pieces of matter swirled around. Ngombe could be the universe, the planets, the performers, and all matter. Nzambi then produced motion, together with the matter which he had produced, started to change and drift aside. So, he produced a being that could traverse the medium and universe between matter and room. Nzambi focused on a set point and gave life up to a being who had been simultaneously man and woman, a manifestation associated with Nzambi, called 20. This spirit is exú-Aluvaiá.[164]

---

[162] "The True History and Faith Behind Voodoo - French Quarter. https://www.frenchquarter.com/true-history-faith-behind-voodoo/. Accessed 15 Aug. 2020.

[163] "The Voodoo Hoodoo Spellbook: Li Grand Zombi. http://voodoohoodoospellbook.blogspot.com/p/serpent-worship.html. Accessed 15 Aug. 2020.

[164] "The Voodoo Hoodoo Spellbook: Li Grand Zombi. http://voodoohoodoospellbook.blogspot.com/p/serpent-worship.html. Accessed 15 Aug. 2020.

Louis Marine provided information about Li Grand Zombi, priest, religious doctor, and elder associated with the New Orleans Voodoo Spiritual Temple:

The Grande Zombie could be the Temple Snake, an element that is defining of Orleans Voodoo and a loa of good stature. The Grande Zombie of New Orleans Voodoo is not mistaken for the Zombie of Haitian Voodoo, which some labeled as a ceremonially animated corpse.[165]

The Temple Snake holds little physical or resemblance that is spiritual this kind of being.[166] The Grande Zombie may fill many roles and accomplish many ritual features.[167] The people considered the Temple Snake is the umbilical cord, the joining between the mother and the child in this Order of Service.[168]

Some people favor venerating Li Grand Zombi by buying a real-time boa-constrictor or python, but they do not suggest this is the live food it requires unless one knows how to take care of one and have the enclosure and willingness to feed. Even though these creatures could become used to consuming frozen mice, rats, or rabbits, it is not the choice that is best. Remember, these serpents grow to be large, plus they can be dangerous.[169]

How does one use a snake in a Voodoo service without being bitten?

[165] The Voodoo Hoodoo Spellbook: Li Grand Zombi.
https://voodoohoodoospellbook.blogspot.com/p/serpent-worship.html
[166] The Voodoo Hoodoo Spellbook: Li Grand Zombi.
https://voodoohoodoospellbook.blogspot.com/p/serpent-worship.html
[167] The Voodoo Hoodoo Spellbook: Li Grand Zombi.
https://voodoohoodoospellbook.blogspot.com/p/serpent-worship.html
[168] "The Voodoo Hoodoo Spellbook: Li Grand Zombi.
http://voodoohoodoospellbook.blogspot.com/p/serpent-worship.html.
Accessed 15 Aug. 2020.
[169] The Voodoo Hoodoo Spellbook: Li Grand Zombi.
https://voodoohoodoospellbook.blogspot.com/p/serpent-worship.html

One way is to be sure that they fed the snake ahead of the service.[170] The other concern is just how familiar the snake is with people and activity. Snakes should be conditioned through publicity to tolerate such stimuli; an eye that is well-trained snake behavior is needed to keep protection for the serpent and the people present. However, the person found the risks of startling the pet or overstimulating it, not feeding it adequately, or allowing an inexperienced person to manage it.[171] It is always superlative to use a snake fetish or doll rather than a live animal and to trust the experience associated with the Voodoo Queen to create out her snake whenever called for within a ritual. Specific practitioners have not any genuine need to gain one of these intelligent creatures.[172]

Making use of Li Grand Zombi and snakes used in Hoodoo, the usage of snake sheds in preparing gris-gris, conjure powders, and natural oils. Power, energy, retribution, and restoration are on the list of attributes associated with the snake in conjure snake's imagery customarily noticed in the event labeled as alive. This ritual is often a condition in which an individual believes someone hoodooed them, and as an outcome, the person may find live things, usually snakes, living within the body. The afflicted person may report being able to feel the snakes crawling around under their epidermis or in their bellies.[173]

Snake conjuring can involve drawing and individual.[174] A proven

---

[170] The Voodoo Hoodoo Spellbook: Li Grand Zombi.
https://voodoohoodoospellbook.blogspot.com/p/serpent-worship.html
[171] The Voodoo Hoodoo Spellbook: Li Grand Zombi.
https://voodoohoodoospellbook.blogspot.com/p/serpent-worship.html
[172] The Voodoo Hoodoo Spellbook: Li Grand Zombi.
https://voodoohoodoospellbook.blogspot.com/p/serpent-worship.html
[173] "The Voodoo Hoodoo Spellbook: Li Grand Zombi.
http://voodoohoodoospellbook.blogspot.com/p/serpent-worship.html.
Accessed 15 Aug. 2020.
[174] The Voodoo Hoodoo Spellbook: Li Grand Zombi.

way they accomplish this is by using hairs from the head and naming all of them for the main one wish.[175] They then place the hairs in a bottle during a mild rainfall, and they permit the container to fill up with rainwater.[176] The bottle may be sealed and kept close to the door of this residence.[177] They allege the hairs to swell up and turn into snakes within a few days. We believe the snake to become so powerful that the one desired cannot withstand the desire to come to the home.[178]

The old-timers became skilled at conjuring; the person needs to get the gift and/or permission from the snake. One way they did it in the past had been through eating the brains of a snake so they could use the knowledge about the serpent in the water. Conjurers would lie down when the person looks at the woods and calls upon the snakes to come and crawl over them. If they could not calmly glance at the serpents in the eyes without flinching, it considered them to be fit to become a conjurer.[179]

No longer solely the coziness and succor spirit of Africans, the faith today known as Voodoo ended up being poised just to take one hell of a star change.[180]

---

https://voodoohoodoospellbook.blogspot.com/p/serpent-worship.html
[175] The Voodoo Hoodoo Spellbook: Li Grand Zombi.
https://voodoohoodoospellbook.blogspot.com/p/serpent-worship.html
[176] The Voodoo Hoodoo Spellbook: Li Grand Zombi.
https://voodoohoodoospellbook.blogspot.com/p/serpent-worship.html
[177] The Voodoo Hoodoo Spellbook: Li Grand Zombi.
https://voodoohoodoospellbook.blogspot.com/p/serpent-worship.html
[178] "The Voodoo Hoodoo Spellbook: Li Grand Zombi.
http://voodoohoodoospellbook.blogspot.com/p/serpent-worship.html.
Accessed 15 Aug. 2020.
[179] "Li Grand Zombi | Dieline. 13 Mar. 2013,
http://www.thedieline.com/blog/2013/3/13/li-grand-zombi.html. Accessed 15 Aug. 2020.
[180] "Li Grand Zombi | Dieline. 13 Mar. 2013,
http://www.thedieline.com/blog/2013/3/13/li-grand-zombi.html. Accessed 15

Scholars touched shortly on Voodoo's influence on the town community whenever speaking about passaging Joey LaCaze, a much-loved and unendingly prolific drummer who was well known for their work behind the system for the renowned Eyehategod Outlaw Order the Mystick Krewe of Clearlight. When he was not pounding out molten sludge grooves or moonlighting in various Solamente electronics jobs, LaCaze performed ceremonial voodoo drumming. When it appeared time to lay their heart to sleep, his household supported the funeral at New Orleans' revered Voodoo Spiritual Temple. LaCaze's friend Anselmo pointed out the ceremony in a meeting, consisting of a priestess who was giving her sermon. "Mike IX Williams stood next to the person. The person scattered blood on that back of the person's head while beating the tambourine. The individual bloodied up their knuckles and virtually destroyed this tambourine. Most took handwritten messages and buried them together with ashes.[181]

The people established the Voodoo Spiritual Temple in 1990 by Priestess Miriam and Priest Oswan Chamani in the quarter that is French on the street from historic Congo Square and straight attached to the square's Voodoo's history.[182] The colonists' Code Noir said that African slaves traditionally had Sundays off during the Spanish and French colonial era.[183] The slaves would go to the square and spend their free time visiting, dancing, and playing music together until stricter American slaveholders ended the practice in

---

Aug. 2020.
[181] "Li Grand Zombi on Behance. 31 Jul. 2012, https://www.behance.net/gallery/4681719/Li-Grand-Zombi. Accessed 15 Aug. 2020.
[182] From Benin to Bourbon Street: A Brief History of Louisiana ....
https://www.vice.com/en_us/article/r7g5ar/from-benin-to-bourbon-street-a-brief-history-of-louisiana-voodoo
[183] From Benin to Bourbon Street: A Brief History of Louisiana ....
https://www.vice.com/en_us/article/r7g5ar/from-benin-to-bourbon-street-a-brief-history-of-louisiana-voodoo

the mid-19th century on those days.[184]

A short walk, Congo Square from the St. Louis Cathedral, where famous voodoo queen Marie Laveau presented community rituals after, they said, attending Catholic Mass in the cathedral. Laveau is one of New Orleans' most elusive and iconic spiritual figures in the 1820s-1860s. She was the daughter of a well-off Creole plantation owner, Charles Laveaux, along with his Haitian servant mistress. She married first free man of color Jacques Paris and then entering a law that is common (or plaçage) with Christophe de Glapion, another no-cost male of color with whom she had fifteen children (including daughter Marie Laveau II, Marie trained her in Voodoo beliefs).[185]

Scholars believed Marie studied "voodoo from fortune-telling" Dr. John (identified as Bayou John and Prince John), students of no-cost Santo Dominican spiritual leader Sanite Dede, who is NOLA's first voodoo queen and reigned supreme from 1822 to 1830 before Laveau usurped her position. The calculating Laveau apprenticed underneath the Congolese hex-breaker Marie Saloppe, working alongside the more experienced voodoo at prominent Midsummer St. John's Eve ceremonies until, hungry for energy, Laveau hexed Salope and drove the older girl insane. During her training, Laveau had kept herself by a hairdresser for the town's social elite; developing a clientele that is dedicated valued her arcane understanding, too, as her hairstyling prowess. Free to manage one other women's consumer, Laveau rose to prominence by 1830, coating her pockets by attempting to sell gris-gris and perpetuating her very own legend as she went. She became well known for her

---

[184] From Benin to Bourbon Street: A Brief History of Louisiana ....
https://www.vice.com/en_us/article/r7g5ar/from-benin-to-bourbon-street-a-brief-history-of-louisiana-voodoo
[185] "Li Grand Zombi on Behance. 31 Jul. 2012,
https://www.behance.net/gallery/4681719/Li-Grand-Zombi. Accessed 15 Aug. 2020.

Voodoo in public, and individuals thought to hold a frightening level of sway on the town's elite.[186]

A catholic influence aided into incorporating Catholicism into a voodoo belief system that had started much earlier in the day. Through its early Francophone influence and despite the conflict inherent in the two religions, Louisiana voodoo in specific stocks, many significant saints and prayers within the Catholic tradition. A move that prefigured Voodoo's in New Orleans in Laveau's later years tells her to have dedicated herself to Catholicism. While a believed fifteen percent of New Orleans natives, however, exercise Voodoo, the religion was riveted into current Catholicism and further diluted by external influences from Wicca, pagan, along with other occult philosophy. It is the central city's mystical fabric but is at risk of becoming merely another visitor attraction.[187]

Luckily, for engaging while the faithful alike, several community institutions perform their best to help keep that magical history alive and give a wide berth to being trapped into the brambles of tourism and technology. Laveau's ghost is held alive by her permanent destination in New Orleans' voodoo history, much tangibly, in the preferred Marie Laveau's House of a Voodoo store on Bourbon Street that serves wandering tourists while offering materials for real professionals. An altar to Baphomet looms over the straight backroom. Individuals could buy charms and incense. The New Orleans Historic Voodoo Museum on Dumaine Street offered an even more complete experience within its halls lined with voodoo

---

[186] "Li Grand Zombi on Behance. 31 Jul. 2012, https://www.behance.net/gallery/4681719/Li-Grand-Zombi. Accessed 15 Aug. 2020.
[187] "Li Grand Zombi on Behance. 31 Jul. 2012, https://www.behance.net/gallery/4681719/Li-Grand-Zombi. Accessed 15 Aug. 2020.

traditions.[188]

---

[188] "Li Grand Zombi on Behance. 31 Jul. 2012, https://www.behance.net/gallery/4681719/Li-Grand-Zombi. Accessed 15 Aug. 2020.

# Chapter 7 Genealogical chart of Marie Catherine Laveaux

Historical Narrative of Marie Catherine Laveau

When Marie Catherine Laveau and her twin sister Marie were born on September 10, 1794, in New Orleans, Louisiana, their father, Charles, was 20, and their mother, Marguerite, was 22. She had nine sons and 11 daughters. She died on June 15, 1881, in her hometown, having lived a long life of 86 years.

**Marie Carene Laveaux-Augustin**
- + 19 Children

**Marie Catherine Laveau**
Spouses
**Jacques Santiago Paris**
- + 4 Spouses

Parents
**Charles Laveaux**
**Marguerite Toussainte Henry**
Locations
Birth: 10 SEP 1794 • New Orleans, LA, USA; Death: 15 JUN 1881 • New Orleans, Louisiana; Burial: 1881 • New Orleans, Orleans Parish, Louisiana, USA; Burial: New Orleans, Orleans Parish, Louisiana, USA; Christening: 16 SEP 1801 • New Orleans, Orleans, Louisiana, United States; Marriage: 1818-09-05 • New Orleans Orleans Louisiana USA; Marriage: 1802 • New Orleans, Orleans, Louisiana, United States; Marriage: 4 AUG 1819 • Saint Louis Cathedral, New Orleans, LA; Marriage: 4 AUG 1819 • New Orleans, Orleans, Louisiana, United States; Marriage: 4 AUG 1819 • Saint Louis Cathedral, New Orleans, LA; Probate: 26 APR 1881 • Orleans, Louisiana, USA; Residence: 1820 • New Orleans, New Orleans City, Louisiana, United States

## Life Story Events

**• 10 SEP 1794**

### Birth

On September 10, 1794, in New Orleans, Louisiana, Marie Cathine Laveau was born to Marguerite Toussainte Henry, age 22, and Charles Laveaux, age 20.[189]

**10 SEP 1794 • New Orleans, LA, USA**

**• 1795 AGE 1**

### Birth and Death of Brother

Her brother Miguel Germelo was born in 1795 and died that same day.

**Miguel Germelo D'Arcantel**

1795–1795

**1795 • New Orleans, Orleans, Louisiana, United States**

**• 10 SEP 1801 AGE 7**

### Cotton in the Deep South

Marie Catherine Laveau was living in Louisiana in 1801 when the cotton crop reigned as the lifeblood to the state's economy.

---

[189] The More You Know About Marie Laveau... | Way Up in the Attic.
https://wayupintheattic.wordpress.com/2015/09/16/the-more-you-know-about-marie-laveau/

○

•      16 SEP

**1801**

AGE 7

## Christening

## 16 SEP 1801 • New Orleans, Orleans, Louisiana, United States

•      16 SEP

**1801**

AGE 7

## baptism Marie Catherine Laveau

○

**16 September 1801**

•      **1802**

## AGE 8

### Marriage

Marie Catherine Laveau married Jacques Santiago Paris in New Orleans, Louisiana, in 1802 when she was eight years old.

### Jacques Santiago Paris

1781–1820

### 1802 • New Orleans, Orleans, Louisiana, United States

• 4 JUL
1803
AGE 8

### The Louisiana Purchase

Marie Catherine Laveau lived in Louisiana around 1803 when the Louisiana Purchase changed its ownership from France to the United States.

○     View             Historical            Insight

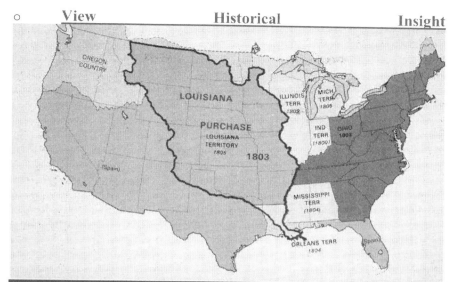

-     3 JAN
## 1804
## AGE 9

### Birth of Half-Sister

Her half-sister Marie Dolores was born on January 3, 1804, in New Orleans, Louisiana, when Marie Catherine was nine years old.

**Marie Dolores Laveaux**

1804–1839

**3 January 1804 • New Orleans, Orleans, Louisiana, United States**

-     30 JUL
## 1805
## AGE 10

### Birth of Brother

Her brother Laurent Charles was born on July 30, 1805, in New Orleans, Louisiana, when Marie Catherine was ten years old.

**Laurent Charles Laveaux**

1805–1890

## 30 JUL 1805 • New Orleans, Orleans, Louisiana, United States

• 30 JUL
**1805**
AGE 10

### Birth of Brother

Her brother Laurent was born on July 30, 1805, in New Orleans, Louisiana, when Marie Catherine was ten years old.

**Laurent Laveau**

1805–1890

## 30 JUL 1805 • New Orleans, Orleans, Louisiana, United States

• 30 JUL
**1805**
AGE 10

### Birth of Half-Brother

Her half-brother Laurent was born on July 30, 1805, in New Orleans, Louisiana, when Marie Catherine was ten years old.

**Laurent Laveau**

1805–1890

## 30 JUL 1805 • New Orleans, Orleans, Louisiana, United States

• 1807
AGE 13

### Marriage

Marie Catherine Laveau married Francois Augustin in 1807 when she was 13 years old.

**Francois Augustin**

1790–1835

## 1807

• ABT
**1809**
AGE 15

## Birth of Sister

Her sister Adelaide was born in 1809 in New Orleans, Louisiana when Marie Catherine was 15 years old.

**Adelaide D'Arcantel**

1809–1815

## ABT 1809 • New Orleans, Orleans, Louisiana, United States

| • | ABT |
|---|---|

**1809**

AGE 15

## Birth of Sister

Her sister Adelaide was born in 1809 when Marie Catherine was 15 years old.

**Adelaide D'Arcantel**

1809–1815

## ABT 1809

| • | ABT |
|---|---|

**1815**

AGE 21

## Death of Sister

Her sister Adelaide died in 1815 when Marie Catherine was 21 years old.

**Adelaide D'Arcantel**

1809–1815

## ABT 1815

| • | 1815 |
|---|---|

AGE 21

## Death of Half-Sister

Her half-sister Marie Henriette died in 1815 in Louisiana when Marie Catherine was 21 years old.

**1815**

| • | 1817 |
|---|---|

AGE 23

**Birth of Daughter**
Her daughter Felicity was born in 1817.
<u>**Felicite Paris**</u>

<u>1817–1824</u>

**1817 • New Orleans**

●      5 SEP
**1818**
AGE 23

**Marriage**
Marie Catherine Laveau married Francois Augustin in New Orleans,
Louisiana, on September 5, 1818, when she was 23 years old.

<u>**Francois Augustin**</u>

<u>1790–1835</u>

**1818-09-05 • New Orleans Orleans Louisiana the USA**

●      10 JUN
**1819**
AGE 24

**Birth of Son**
Her son Lorenzo was born on June 10, 1819.
<u>**Lorenzo Auguste**</u>

<u>1819–</u>

## 6/10/1819 • New Orleans

- **4 AUG 1819 AGE 24**

### Marriage

Marie Catherine Laveau married Jacques Santiago Paris in New Orleans, Louisiana, on August 4, 1819, when she was 24 years old.

### Jacques Santiago Paris

1781–1820

## 4 AUG 1819 • Saint Louis Cathedral, New Orleans, LA

- **4 AUG 1819 AGE 24**

### Marriage

Marie Catherine Laveau married Santyaque Santiago "Jacques" in New Orleans, Louisiana, on August 4, 1819, when she was 24 years old.

## Santyaque Santiago "Jacques"

### 1781–1820

### 4 AUG 1819 • New Orleans, Orleans, Louisiana, United States

- **4 AUG 1819 AGE 24**

### Marriage

Marie Catherine Laveau married Santyaque Santiago "Jacques" in New Orleans, Louisiana, on August 4, 1819, when she was 24 years old.

## Santyaque Santiago "Jacques"

### 1781–1820

### 4 AUG 1819 • Saint Louis Cathedral, New Orleans, LA

- **21 DEC**

## 1820
### AGE 26
### Birth of Daughter
Her daughter Marie Henriette was born on December 21, 1820.
**Marie Henriette Augusto**

1820–

**12/21/1820 • New Orleans**

## • 1820
### AGE 26

### Residence
Marie Catherine Laveau lived in New Orleans, Louisiana, in 1820.

**1820 • New Orleans, New Orleans City, Louisiana, United States**

## • 1820
### AGE 26
### Death of Husband
Her husband, Santyaque, died in 1820 in New Orleans, Louisiana, at 39. They had been married for one year.
**Santyaque Santiago "Jacques"**

1781–1820

**1820 • New Orleans, Orleans, Louisiana, USA**

## • 1820
### AGE 26
### Birth of Son
Her son Francois was born in 1820.

# Francois DeGlapion

1820–

**1820**

- **16 AUG**
**1822**
AGE 27

**Birth of Daughter**
Her daughter Francisca was born on August 16, 1822.
Francisca Augusto

1822–

**8/16/1822 • New Orleans**

- **13 FEB**
**1823**
AGE 28

**Birth of Daughter**
Her daughter Marie-Angelie was born on February 13, 1823.
Marie-Angelie Paris

1823–1830

**ABT 13 FEB 1823**

- **13 FEB**
**1823**
AGE 28

**Death of Daughter**
Her daughter Marie Angelie died on February 13, 1823, in New Orleans, Louisiana, when she was less than a year old.
Marie Angelie Paris

1823–1823

**13 Feb 1823 • New Orleans, Orleans, Louisiana, USA**

- **1823**
AGE 29

**Birth of Daughter**

Her daughter Marie Angelie was born in 1823.
**Marie Angelie Paris**

1823–1823

**1823 • New Orleans**

| • | 1 SEP |
| --- | --- |
| **1824** | |
| AGE 29 | |

**Birth of Son**

On September 1, 1824. Marie Angelie Paris had a son[190]
**Joseph Auguste**

1824–

**9-1-1824 • New Orleans**

| • | 15 NOV |
| --- | --- |
| **1824** | |
| AGE 30 | |

**Birth of Daughter**

Her daughter Felicite was born on November 15, 1824.
**Felicite Paris**

1824–1830

**ABT 15 NOV 1824**

| • | 15 NOV |
| --- | --- |
| **1824** | |
| AGE 30 | |

**Death of Daughter**

Her daughter Felicitie died on November 15, 1824, in New Orleans, Louisiana, at 7.

---

[190] Relatives, In-Laws, and Possible Cousins of Gary Kueber ....
http://kueber.us/p1063.htm

## Felicite Paris

1817–1824

### 15 Nov 1824 • New Orleans, Orleans, Louisiana, USA

- 31 JUL
**1825**
AGE 30

**Death of Mother**
Her mother, Marguerite Toussainte, died on July 31, 1825, in New Orleans, Louisiana, at 53.
Marguerite Toussainte Henry

1772–1825

### 31 JUL 1825 • New Orleans, Orleans, Louisiana, USA

- 1825
AGE 31

**Death of Mother**
Her mother, Marguerite Toussainte, died in 1825 in New Orleans, Louisiana, at 53.
Marguerite Toussainte Henry

1772–1825

### 1825 • New Orleans, LA

- 23 APR
**1826**
AGE 31

**Birth of Son**
Her son Felix was born on April 23, 1826.
Felix Auguste

1826–

### 4-23-1826 • New Orleans

- 10 SEP

## 1829
## AGE 35
### Death of Daughter
Her daughter Marie-Louise "Caroline" died on September 10, 1829.
### Marie-Louise "Caroline" Glapion

–1829

## 10 SEP 1829
## •       ABT
## 1830
## AGE 36
### Death of Daughter
Her daughter Marie-Angelie died in 1830 at 7.
### Marie-Angelie Paris

1823–1830

## ABT 1830
## •       ABT
## 1830
## AGE 36
### Death of Daughter
Her daughter Felicite died in 1830 at 6.
### Felicite Paris

1824–1830

## ABT 1830
## •       8 SEP
## 1831
## AGE 36
### Birth of Son
Her son Francois was born on September 8, 1831.
### Francois Augusto

1831–1831

## 9-8-1831 • New Orleans

- **28 SEP**
**1831**
**AGE 37**

**Death of Son**

Her son Francois died on September 28, 1831, when he was less than a year old.

**Francois Augusto**

1831–1831

## 9-28-1831 • New Orleans

- **22 SEP**
**1833**
**AGE 39**

**Birth of Son**

Her son Maurice Christophe was born on September 22, 1833, in Louisiana.

**Maurice Christophe Glapion**

1833–

## 22 SEP 1833 • LA, Orleans Parish, New Orleans

- **18 MAY**
**1834**
**AGE 39**

**Death of Son**

Her son François-Auguste died on May 18, 1834.

**François-Auguste Glapion**

–1834

## 18 MAY 1834

- **27 SEP**
**1835**
**AGE 41**

**Death of Father**

Her father Charles died on September 27, 1835, in New Orleans,

Louisiana, at 61.

## Charles Laveaux

1774–1835

## 27 SEP 1835 • New Orleans, Orleans, Louisiana, USA

- **27 SEP 1835**
**AGE 41**

**Death of Father**

Her father, Charles, died on September 27, 1835, in New Orleans, Louisiana, at 60.

## Charles Laveau Trudeau

1775–1835

## 27 SEP 1835 • New Orleans, Orleans, Louisiana, United States

- **27 SEP 1835**
**AGE 41**

**Death of Brother**

Her brother Charles died on September 27, 1835, in New Orleans, Louisiana, when Marie Catherine was 41 years old.

## Charles Laveaux

1774–1835

## 27 SEP 1835 • New Orleans, Orleans, Louisiana, USA

•     27 SEP
**1835**
AGE 41

### Death of Brother

Her brother Charles died on September 27, 1835, in New Orleans, Louisiana, when Marie Catherine was 41 years old.

**Charles Laveaux**

1774–1835

## 27 SEP 1835 • New Orleans, Louisiana, USA

•     27 SEP
**1835**
AGE 41

### Death of Brother

Her brother Charles died on September 27, 1835, in New Orleans, Louisiana, when Marie Catherine was 41 years old.

**Charles Laveaux**

1774–1835

## 27 SEP 1835 • New Orleans City, Orleans, Louisiana

•     6 MAR
**1836**
AGE 41

### Birth of Daughter

Her daughter Marie Philomène was born on March 6, 1836, in New Orleans, Louisiana.

## Marie Philomène Glapion

1836–1897

**6 MAR 1836 • New Orleans, Orleans, Louisiana, USA**
- **1837**
AGE 43
**Marie Laveau**

Depiction of the famed Voodoo Priestess by artist George Catlin.

## 1837

**22 JUN 1839 AGE 44**

### Death of Half-Sister
Her half-sister Marie Dolores died on June 22, 1839, when Marie Catherine was 44 years old.
**Marie Dolores Laveaux**

1804–1839

### 22 June 1839 • Paris, France

**NOV 1839 AGE 45**

### Birth of Son
Her son Auguste was born in November 1839 in Louisiana.
**Auguste Glapion**

1839–1840

### NOV 1839 • LA, Orleans Parish, New Orleans

**9 AUG 1840 AGE 45**

### Death of Son
Her son Auguste died on August 9, 1840, in Louisiana when he was less than a year old.
**Auguste Glapion**

1839–1840

### 9 AUG 1840 • LA, Orleans Parish, New Orleans

**8 JAN 1845 AGE 50**

### Death of Son
Her son Archange died on January 8, 1845.

## Archange Glapion

### –1845

### 8 JAN 1845

- **1848**

AGE 54

**Death of Sister**

Her sister Marie Josephe died in 1848 when Marie Catherine was 54 years old.

## Marie Josephe Pouponne Diaz

### 1786–1848

### 1848

- **26 JUN**

**1855**

AGE 60

**Death of Husband**

Her husband, Jean Christophe's Duminy, died on June 26, 1855, in New Orleans, Louisiana, at 66.

## Jean Christophe' Duminy DeGlapion

### 1789–1855

### 26 JUN 1855 • New Orleans, Orleans, Louisiana, USA

- **1860**

AGE 66

**Residence**
**1860**

- **1870**

AGE 76

**Residence**
**1870**

- **15 JUN**

## 1881
### AGE 86
### Death

Marie Catherine Laveau died on June 15, 1881, in New Orleans, Louisiana, when she was 86 years old.

**15 JUN 1881 • New Orleans, Louisiana**

### • 1881
### Burial

**1881 • New Orleans, Orleans Parish, Louisiana, USA**

### •
### Burial

## New Orleans, Orleans Parish, Louisiana, USA

- **26 APR 1881**
  AGE 86

## Probate

## 26 APR 1881 • Orleans, Louisiana, USA

- **15 JUN 1881**
  AGE 86

## Death Certificate

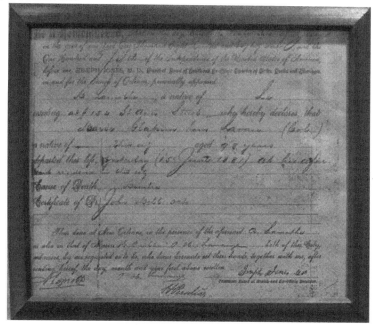

## 15 June 1881

● 28 JUN
1881
AGE 86

## 18810628 Wilmington, Delaware Daily_Gazette_p4

The negroes of Richmond, Va., are greatly excited to-day by the announcement of the possible fatal illness of the Rev. John Jasper, the negro preacher, who was made famous two years ago by preaching a sermon in which he argued that the sun, and not the earth, moves. A large number of the more illiterate negroes have long looked upon Jasper as a sort of prophet, and regarding him with superstitious awe. He is a pastor of Mount Zion Church, in the outskirts of the city, and has the largest congregation of any preacher in the South and one of the largest in the United States, it numbering about 4,000.

The colony of negro Voudous in and around New Orleans celebrated St. John's Eve on last Thursday evening, convened in a lonely grove, and in honor of the memory of their late queen, Marie Lavau, went through the weird vou-fire ceremonies. A large bon-fire was built, around and through which they danced and jumped and chanted melancholy tunes until daylight.

## 28 Jun 1881

● JUN
1881
AGE 86

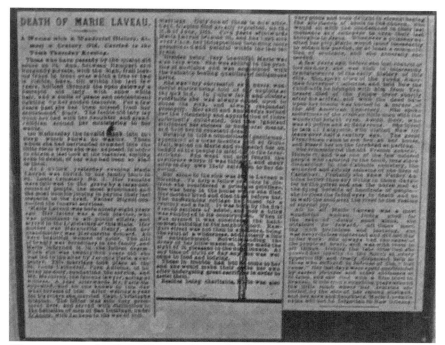

**Newspaper Article Regarding the Death of Marie Laveau**

o

## June 1881
## Marriage

Marie Catherine Laveau married Jean Christophe' Duminy DeGlapion.

## Jean Christophe' Duminy DeGlapion

1789–1855

Genealogical Chart concerning Marie Catherine Laveau

**Marie Catherine Laveau** 1794-1881

*3rd great-grandmother*

Marie Carene Laveaux-Augustin

*Daughter of Marie Catherine Laveau*

Rosie Marie (Choctaw enrollment No.10807) George, Wilson, Black, Randolph -1959

*Daughter of Marie Carene Laveaux-Augustin*

Alberta Collins Walker Flint Jackson 1904-2000

*Daughter of Rosie Marie (Choctaw enrollment No.10807) George, Wilson, Black, Randolph*

Rosetta Walker-Bell-Dantzler 1924-1998

*Daughter of Alberta Collins Walker Flint Jackson*

**Sir Kenneth Dantzler Corbin, Duke**

*You are the son of Rosetta Walker-Bell-Dantzler*

A historical narrative of Charles LaVeau, the father of Marie Catherine Laveau

When Charles Laveaux was born in 1774 in New Orleans, Louisiana, his father, Charles, was -1, and his mother, Marguerite, was 2. Charles Laveaux married three times and had four sons and three daughters.[191] He died on September 27, 1835, in his hometown at 61.

## Marie Catherine Laveau
-    + 5 Children

## Charles Laveaux
Spouses

## Marie Francoise Fanchon Dupart
-    + 2 Spouses

Parents

## Charles Laveau Trudeau
## Marguerite Toussainte Henry
Locations

Birth: about 1774 • New Orleans, Orleans, Louisiana, United States; Death: 27 SEP 1835 • New Orleans, Orleans, Louisiana, USA; Marriage: 2 August 1802 • New Orleans, Orleans, Louisiana, United States; Marriage: 2 AUG 1802 • New Orleans, Orleans, Louisiana, United States; Marriage: 2 AUG 1802 • New Orleans, Orleans, Louisiana, United States; Marriage: 2 AUG 1802 • New Orleans, LA; Probate: Orleans, Louisiana, USA; Residence: Arkansas, USA; Residence: 1791 • New Orleans, Orleans Parish, LA; Residence: 1810 • New Orleans, Orleans, Louisiana, United States

## Life Story Events
-    ABOUT

---

[191] Frederick Gottlieb Hoberg (1826-1903) - Find A Grave Memorial. https://www.findagrave.com/memorial/37216569/frederick-gottlieb-hoberg

## 1774
### Birth
Charles Laveaux was born in 1774 in New Orleans, Louisiana, to Marguerite Toussainte Henry, age 2, and Charles Laveau Trudeau, age -1.

**about 1774 • New Orleans, Orleans, Louisiana, United States**

## • 4 JUL 1776 AGE 2

### The Declaration of Independence
Charles Laveaux was living in the 13 provinces at one of the most prominent turning moments in the United States of American history—the signing of the Declaration of Independence.[192]

---

[192] The Declaration of Independence - Ancestry Insights.
https://www.ancestry.com/contextux/historicalinsights/declaration-independence/persons/12561615223:1030:27038219

**1776**

AGE 2

**Birth of Brother**

His brother Nicolas was born in 1776 in New Orleans, Louisiana, when Charles was two years old.

Nicolas Laveau

1776–

## 1776 • New Orleans, Orleans, Louisiana, United States

• 19 MAR
**1781**
AGE 7

**Birth of Half-Sister**

His half-sister Charlotte was born on March 19, 1781, in New Orleans, Louisiana, when Charles was seven years old.

**Charlotte Trudeau**

1781–

## 19 MAR 1781 • New Orleans, Orleans, Louisiana, United States

• 19 MAR
**1781**
AGE 7

**Birth of Half-Sister**

His half-sister Charlotte was born on March 19, 1781, in New Orleans, Louisiana, when Charles was seven years old.

**19 MAR 1781**

• 1786
AGE 12

**Birth of Sister**

His sister Marie Josephe was born in 1786 in New Orleans, Louisiana, when Charles was 12 years old.

**Marie Josephe Pouponne Diaz**

1786–1848

## 1786 • New Orleans, Orleans, Louisiana, United States

• 2 AUG
**1787**
AGE 13

**Birth of Half-Sister**

His half-sister Maria Josefa was born on August 2, 1787, in New Orleans, Louisiana, when Charles was 13 years old.

**Maria Josefa Trudeau**

1787–

## 2 AUG 1787 • New Orleans, Orleans, Louisiana, United States

- **2 AUG 1787 AGE 13**

### Birth of Half-Sister

His half-sister Maria Josefa was born on August 2, 1787, in New Orleans, Louisiana, when Charles was 13 years old.

**2 AUG 1787**

- **1789 AGE 15**

## Plan of the City of New Orleans and the Adjacent Plantations compiled per an Ordinance of the Illustrious Ministry

Title: Copy and Translation from the Original Spanish Plan Dated 1798, Showing the City of New Orleans, Its Fortifications And Environs April 1875; Creator Trudeau, Carlos Laveau, 1748-1816 Credit The Historic New Orleans Collection, Gift of Boyd Cruise and Harold Schilke Description: Copy of a map "Plan of the City of New Orleans and the Adjacent Plantations compiled per an Ordinance of the Illustrious Ministry and Royal Charter, 24 December 1789, signed Carlos Trudeau. The map shows fortified French Quarter city and the Mississippi River, out to the area, including Lake Pontchartrain. [193]

---

193

Image from The Historic New Orleans Collection (http://www.hnoc.org)

**1789**

**1791**

AGE 17

### Residence
Charles Laveaux lived in New Orleans, Louisiana, in 1791.

## 1791 • New Orleans, Orleans Parish, LA

| • 7 DEC 1793 AGE 19 |
| --- |

**Birth of Half-Sister**

His half-sister Maria was born on December 7, 1793, in New Orleans, Louisiana, when Charles was 19 years old.

**Maria Trudeau**

1793–

## 7 DEC 1793 • New Orleans, Orleans, Louisiana, United States

| • 7 DEC 1793 AGE 19 |
| --- |

**Birth of Half-Sister**

His half-sister Maria was born on December 7, 1793, in New Orleans, Louisiana, when Charles was 19 years old.
**7 DEC 1793**

| • 10 SEP 1794 AGE 20 |
| --- |

**Birth of Daughter**

His daughter Marie Catherine was born on September 10, 1794, in New Orleans, Louisiana.

## Marie Catherine Laveau

### 1794–1881

**10 SEP 1794 • New Orleans, LA, USA**

- **10 SEP 1794**
  AGE 20

**Birth of Sister**

His sister Marie Catherine was born on September 10, 1794, in New Orleans, Louisiana, when Charles was 20 years old.

## Marie Catherine Laveau

### 1794–1881

**10 SEP 1794 • New Orleans, LA, USA**

- **10 SEP 1794**
  AGE 20

**Birth of Sister**

His sister Marie was born on September 10, 1794, in New Orleans, Louisiana, when Charles was 20 years old.

## Marie (Laveaux) Laveau

### 1794–1881

**10 SEP 1794 • New Orleans, Orleans, Louisiana, United States**

- **1794**
  AGE 20

**Birth of Son**

His son Nicolas was born in 1794 in New Orleans, Louisiana.

## Nicolas Laveau

### 1794–

## 1794 • New Orleans, Orleans, Louisiana, United States

**• 1794**
**AGE 20**

### Birth of Half-Brother

His half-brother Nicolas, the son of Charles Laveaux and Marguerite Toussainte Henry, was born in 1794 in New Orleans, Louisiana, when Charles was 20 years old.

**Nicolas Laveau**

1794–

## 1794 • New Orleans, Orleans, Louisiana, United States

**• 1794**
**AGE 20**

### The Dedication of St. Louis Cathedral

When the newly constructed St. Louis Cathedral was dedicated to New Orleans in 1794, Charles Laveaux may have attended the ceremony.

**• 1794**
**AGE 20**

### The invention of the Cotton Gin

In 1794, Southerners like Charles Laveaux of New Orleans, Louisiana, heard talk of a new machine that could clean cotton faster than any man.

**1795**
AGE 21

**Birth and Death of Son**
His son Miguel Germelo was born in 1795 and died that same day.
**Miguel Germelo D'Arcantel**

1795–1795

**1795 • New Orleans, Orleans, Louisiana, United States**

**1795**
AGE 21

**Birth and Death of Half-Brother**
His half-brother Miguel Germelo was born in 1795 and died that
same day.
**Miguel Germelo D'Arcantel**

1795–1795

**1795 • New Orleans, Orleans, Louisiana, United States**

**2 AUG
1802**
AGE 28

**Marriage**
Charles Laveaux married Marie Francoise Fanchon Dupart in New
Orleans, Louisiana, on August 2, 1802, when he was 28 years old.

## Marie Francoise Fanchon Dupart

-1824

## 2 August 1802 • New Orleans, Orleans, Louisiana, United States

- **2 AUG 1802 AGE 28**

## Marriage

Charles Laveaux married Marguerite Toussainte Henry in New Orleans, Louisiana, on August 2, 1802, when he was 28 years old.

## Marguerite Toussainte Henry

1772-1825

## 2 AUG 1802 • New Orleans, Orleans, Louisiana, United States

- **2 AUG**

## 1802
## AGE 28

### Marriage

Charles Laveaux married Marie Francoise Fanchon Dupart in New Orleans, Louisiana, on August 2, 1802, when he was 28 years old.

### Marie Francoise Fanchon Dupart

1784–1824

### 2 AUG 1802 • New Orleans, Orleans, Louisiana, United States

### • 2 AUG
### 1802
### AGE 28

### Marriage

Charles Laveaux married Marie Francoise Fanchon Dupart in New Orleans, Louisiana, on August 2, 1802, when he was 28 years old.

## Marie Francoise Fanchon Dupart

1784–1824

### 2 AUG 1802 • New Orleans, LA

- **3 JAN 1804**
  **AGE 30**

**Birth of Daughter**

His daughter Marie Dolores was born on January 3, 1804, in New Orleans, Louisiana.

**Marie Dolores Laveaux**

1804–1839

### 3 January 1804 • New Orleans, Orleans, Louisiana, United States

- **30 JUL 1805**
  **AGE 31**

**Birth of Son**

His son Laurent Charles was born on July 30, 1805, in New Orleans, Louisiana.

**Laurent Charles Laveaux**

1805–1890

### 30 JUL 1805 • New Orleans, Orleans, Louisiana, United States

- **30 JUL 1805**
  **AGE 31**

**Birth of Brother**

His brother Laurent was born on July 30, 1805, in New Orleans, Louisiana, when Charles was 31 years old.

**Laurent Laveau**

1805–1890

## 30 JUL 1805 • New Orleans, Orleans, Louisiana, United States

- 30 JUL
**1805**
AGE 31

**Birth of Brother**
His brother Laurent was born on July 30, 1805, in New Orleans, Louisiana, when Charles was 31 years old.
**Laurent Laveau**

1805–1890

## 30 JUL 1805 • New Orleans, Orleans, Louisiana, United States

- 30 JUL
**1805**
AGE 31

**Birth of Half-Brother**
His half-brother Laurent Charles, the son of Charles Laveaux and Marguerite Toussainte Henry, was born on July 30, 1805, in New Orleans, Louisiana, when Charles was 31 years old.
**Laurent Charles Laveaux**

1805–1890

## 30 JUL 1805 • New Orleans, Orleans, Louisiana, United States

- ABT
**1809**
AGE 35

**Birth of Daughter**
His daughter Adelaide was born in 1809 in New Orleans, Louisiana.
**Adelaide D'Arcantel**

1809–1815

## ABT 1809 • New Orleans, Orleans, Louisiana, United States

- ABT
**1809**
AGE 35

## Birth of Sister

His sister Adelaide was born in 1809 in New Orleans, Louisiana, when Charles was 35 years old.

### Adelaide D'Arcantel

## 1809–1815

## ABT 1809 • New Orleans, Orleans, Louisiana, United States

| • | 1809 |
|---|---|
| AGE 35 | |

## Charles Trudeau Letters At HNOC

CHARLES TRUDEAU LETTERS

| ID Number: | 94-35-L |
|---|---|
| Title: | Charles Trudeau Letters |
| Item Status: | Permanent Collection    Legal Status: Permanent Collection |
| Object Name: | correspondence |
| Date: | 1809 |
| Object Description | Manuscript letters by Louisiana surveyor Charles Trudeau explaining Spanish methods for surveying Louisiana. 3 letters, English and French, 3 items |
| Title Type: | assigned |
| Extent: | 3 items |
| Collection Theme(s): | Geography and Land Tenure |
| Subjects: | Trudeau, Carlos Laveau, 1749-1816 |
| Other Number: | Non-Collection Number N940420.2 |
| Permalink: | http://hnoc.minisisinc.com/thnoc/catalog/1/157547 |

## 1809

| • | 1810 |
|---|---|
| AGE 36 | |

## Residence

Charles Laveaux lived in New Orleans, Louisiana, in 1810.

## 1810 • New Orleans, Orleans, Louisiana, United States

| • | ABT |
|---|---|

**1815**
AGE 41
**Death of Daughter**
His daughter Adelaide died in 1815 at 6.
<u>**Adelaide D'Arcantel**</u>

<u>1809–1815</u>

**ABT 1815**
•    ABT
**1815**
AGE 41
**Death of Sister**
His sister Adelaide died in 1815 when Charles was 41 years old.
<u>**Adelaide D'Arcantel**</u>

<u>1809–1815</u>

**ABT 1815**
•    1815
AGE 41
**Death of Half-Sister**
His half-sister Marie Henriette died in 1815 in Louisiana when Charles was 41 years old.
<u>**Marie Henriette Laveau Trudeau**</u>

<u>–1815</u>

**1815 • Louisiana, United States**
•    1815
AGE 41
**Death of Half-Sister**
His half-sister Marie Henriette died in 1815 in Louisiana when Charles was 41 years old.
**1815**
•    23 JUN
**1824**
AGE 50

**Death of Wife**

His wife Marie Francoise Fanchon died on June 23, 1824, in New Orleans, Louisiana. They had been married for 21 years.
**Marie Francoise Fanchon Dupart**

–1824

**23 June 1824 • New Orleans, Orleans, Louisiana**

| • | 31 JUL |
|---|---|
| **1825** | |
| AGE 51 | |

**Death of Mother**

His mother, Marguerite Toussainte, died on July 31, 1825, in New Orleans, Louisiana, at 53.
**Marguerite Toussainte Henry**

1772–1825

**31 JUL 1825 • New Orleans, Orleans, Louisiana, USA**

| • | 31 JUL |
|---|---|
| **1825** | |
| AGE 51 | |

**Death of Wife**

His wife, Marguerite Toussainte, died on July 31, 1825, in New Orleans, Louisiana, at 53. They had been married for 22 years.
**Marguerite Toussainte Henry**

1772–1825

**31 JUL 1825 • New Orleans, Orleans, Louisiana, USA**

| • | 1825 |
|---|---|
| AGE 51 | |

**Death of Mother**

His mother, Marguerite Toussainte, died in 1825 in New Orleans, Louisiana, at 53.

## Marguerite Toussainte Henry

1772–1825

### 1825 • New Orleans, LA

- **1825**

AGE 51

**Death of Wife**

His wife, Marguerite Toussainte, died in 1825 in New Orleans, Louisiana, at 53. They had been married for 23 years.

## Marguerite Toussainte Henry

1772–1825

### 1825 • New Orleans, LA

- **27 SEP 1835**

AGE 61

**Death of Father**

His father, Charles, died on September 27, 1835, in New Orleans, Louisiana, at 60.

## Charles Laveau Trudeau

1775–1835

### 27 SEP 1835 • New Orleans, Orleans, Louisiana, United States

- **27 SEP 1835**

AGE 61

### Death

Charles Laveaux died on September 27, 1835, in New Orleans, Louisiana, when he was 61 years old.

## 27 SEP 1835 • New Orleans, Orleans, Louisiana, USA

● **1854**
AGE 80

## Lafayette Park

Designed by Charles Laveau Trudeau

**1854**

●

## Residence

Charles Laveaux lived in Arkansas.

## Arkansas, USA

- 

## Probate

## Orleans, Louisiana, USA

The historical narrative of Carlos "Charles" Laveau Trudeau

When Carlos "Charles" Laveau Trudeau was born on December 1, 1742, in New Orleans, Louisiana, his father, Jean, was 23, and his mother, Marie-Anne, was 21. He had one son with Marguerite D'Arcantel Henry. Carlos "Charles" married Charlotte Perrault, and they had three children together. He died on October 6, 1816, in New Orleans, Louisiana, at 73.

Children
**Charles Laveau Trudeau**
• + 3 Children

**Carlos "Charles" Laveau Trudeau, Surveyor General of Spanish Louisiana; Acting Mayor (1812)**

Spouses
**Charlotte Perrault**
• + 1 Spouse

Parents
**Jean Baptiste Laveau Trudeau**
**Marie-Anne Carriere**

Locations
Birth: 1 Dec 1742 • New Orleans, Orleans, Louisiana, United States; Death: 6 October 1816 • New Orleans, Orleans, Louisiana, United States; Marriage: 24 Jan 1780 • New Orleans, Orleans, Louisiana

**Life Story Events**

• 1 DEC 1742

**Birth**
Carlos "Charles" Laveau Trudeau was born on December 1, 1742, in New Orleans, Louisiana, to Marie-Anne Carriere, age 21, and Jean Baptiste Laveau Trudeau, age 23.

## 1 Dec 1742 • New Orleans, Orleans, Louisiana, United States

• 3 APR
**1744**
AGE 1

### Death of Half-Sister

His half-sister Marie died on April 3, 1744, in Montréal, Quebec, Canada, when Carlos "Charles" Laveau was one year old.
**Marie Trudeau**

1672–1744

### 3 APR 1744 • Montréal, Quebec, Canada

• 3 MAY
**1745**
AGE 2

### Death of Half-Brother

His half-brother Joseph died on May 3, 1745, in Montréal, Quebec, Canada, when Carlos "Charles" Laveau was two years old.
**Joseph Trudeau**

1682–1745

### 3 MAY 1745 • Montréal, Quebec, Canada

• 26 MAR
**1746**
AGE 3

### Birth of Half-Brother

His half-brother Theodore was born on March 26, 1746, in New Orleans, Louisiana, when Carlos "Charles" Laveau was three years old.

## Theodore Trudeau

1746–

## 26 Mar 1746 • New Orleans, Orleans, Louisiana, United States

| • | 7 JUL |
| 1747 | |
| AGE 4 | |

### Birth of Half-Brother

His half-brother Etienne was born on July 7, 1747, in New Orleans, Louisiana, when Carlos "Charles" Laveau was four years old.

## Etienne Trudeau

1747–

## 7 Jul 1747 • New Orleans, Orleans, Louisiana, United States

| • | 12 FEB |
| 1748 | |
| AGE 5 | |

### Death of Half-Brother

His half-brother Étienne died on February 12, 1748, in Chambly, Quebec, Canada, when Carlos "Charles" Laveau was five years old.

## Étienne Trudeau

1667–1748

## 12 FEB 1748 • Chambly, Quebec, Canada

| • | 28 NOV |
| 1748 | |
| AGE 5 | |

### Birth of Brother

His brother Zenon was born on November 28, 1748, in New Orleans, Louisiana, when Carlos "Charles" Laveau was five years old.

## Zenon Trudeau

1748–1813

## 28 NOV 1748 • New Orleans, LA, USA

| • | 28 NOV |
|---|---|
| **1748** | |
| AGE 5 | |

**Birth of Half-Brother**

His half-brother Zenon was born on November 28, 1748, in New Orleans, Louisiana, when Carlos "Charles" Laveau was five years old.

**Zenon Trudeau**

1748–1813

## 28 NOV 1748 • New Orleans, Louisiana

| • | 23 JUL |
|---|---|
| **1750** | |
| AGE 7 | |

**Birth of Half-Sister**

His half-sister Andree Rosalie was born on July 23, 1750, in New Orleans, Louisiana, when Carlos "Charles" Laveau was seven years old.

**Andree Rosalie Trudeau**

1750–

## 23 Jul 1750 • New Orleans, Orleans, Louisiana, United States

| • | 12 FEB |
|---|---|
| **1753** | |
| AGE 10 | |

**Death of Half-Brother**

His half-brother Toussaint died on February 12, 1753, in Longueuil, Quebec, Canada, when Carlos "Charles" Laveau was 10 Years old.

**Toussaint Trudeau**

1676–1753

## 12 FEB 1753 • Longueuil, Quebec, Canada

| • | 16 JUN |
|---|---|

## 1754
## AGE 11

**Death of Half-Brother**

His half-brother Jean-Baptiste died on June 16, 1754, in Terrebonne, Quebec, Canada, when Carlos "Charles" Laveau was 11 years old.
<u>Jean-Baptiste Trudeau</u>

<u>1680–1754</u>

**16 JUN 1754 • Terrebonne, Quebec**

## •        1755
## AGE 13

**Birth of Half-Brother**

His half-brother Charles was born in 1755 in New Orleans, Louisiana when Carlos "Charles" Laveau was 13 years old.

<u>Charles Trudeau dit Laveaux Surveyor General of Spanish Louisiana</u>

<u>1755–1816</u>

**1755 • New Orleans, Orleans, Louisiana, United States**

## •        22 MAR
## 1758
## AGE 15

**Death of Half-Brother**

His half-brother Louis died on March 22, 1758, in Varennes, Quebec, Canada, when Carlos "Charles" Laveau was 15 Years old.
<u>Louis Trudeau</u>

<u>1687–1758</u>

**22 MAR 1758 • Ile Saint-Thérese, Varennès, Québec, Canada**

## •        22 MAR

## 1758
### AGE 15
**Death of Half-Brother**

His half-brother Bertrand died on March 22, 1758, in Varennes, Quebec, Canada, when Carlos "Charles" Laveau was 15 Years old.
**Bertrand Trudeau**

1687–1758

**22 Mar 1758 • Varennes, Quebec, Canada**

| • | 14 JUN |
|---|---|

## 1759
### AGE 16
**Death of Half-Brother**

His half-brother Bertrand died on June 14, 1759, in Montréal, Quebec, Canada, when Carlos "Charles" Laveau was 16 years old.
**Bertrand Trudeau**

1689–1759

**14 JUN 1759 • Montréal, Quebec, Canada**

| • | 10 JUN |
|---|---|

## 1772
### AGE 29
**Death of Father**

His father, Jean Baptiste, died on June 10, 1772, in New Orleans, Louisiana, at 53.
**Jean Baptiste Laveau Trudeau**

1719–1772

**10 June 1772 • New Orleans, Orleans Parish, Louisiana, USA**

| • | 10 JUN |
|---|---|

## 1772
### AGE 29
**Death of Mother**

His mother, Marie-Anne, died on June 10, 1772, in New Orleans, Louisiana, at 51.

## Marie-Anne Carriere

1721–1694

### 10 Jun 1772 • New Orleans, Orleans Parish, Louisiana, USA

- **10 JUN 1772**
**AGE 29**

**Death of Mother**

His mother, Marianne, died on June 10, 1772, in New Orleans, Louisiana, at 43.

## Marianne Carierre

1729–1772

### 10 Jun 1772 • New Orleans, Orleans Parish, Louisiana, USA

- **ABT 1775**
**AGE 33**

**Birth of Son**

His son Charles was born in 1775 in New Orleans, Louisiana.

## Charles Laveau Trudeau

1775–1835

### ABT 1775 • New Orleans, Orleans, Louisiana, United States

- **24 JAN 1780**
**AGE 37**

## Marriage

Carlos "Charles" Laveau Trudeau married Charlotte Perrault in New Orleans, Louisiana, on January 24, 1780, when he was 37 years old.

## Charlotte Perrault

1760–1824

### 24 Jan 1780 • New Orleans, Orleans, Louisiana

**• 1785**

AGE 43

**Birth of Daughter**

His daughter Marie Celestine Laveau was born in 1785 in New Orleans, Louisiana.

**Marie Celestine Laveau Trudeau**

1785–1858

### 1785 • New Orleans Parish, Louisiana

**• 1787**

AGE 45

**Birth of Daughter**

His daughter Josephine Laveau was born in 1787 in New Orleans, Louisiana.

**Josephine Laveau Trudeau**

1787–1849

### 1787 • New Orleans, Louisiana

**• 7 DEC 1793**

AGE 51

**Birth of Daughter**

His daughter Maria Laveau Mannette was born on December 7, 1793, in New Orleans, Louisiana.

<u>Maria Laveau Mannette Trudeau</u>

<u>1793–1858</u>

## 7 Dec 1793 • New Orleans, Louisiana

| • | 5 NOV |
| --- | --- |
| **1807** | |
| AGE 64 | |

**Death of Half-Brother**

His half-brother Jean Louis Marie died on November 5, 1807, in New Orleans, Louisiana, when Carlos "Charles" Laveau was 64 years old.

<u>Jean Louis Marie Trudeau</u>

<u>1742–1807</u>

## 5 Nov 1807 • New Orleans, Orleans, Louisiana, United States

| • | 12 SEP |
| --- | --- |
| **1813** | |
| AGE 70 | |

**Death of Brother**

His brother Zenon died on September 12, 1813, in St Charles, Louisiana, when Carlos "Charles" Laveau was 70 years old.

<u>Zenon Trudeau</u>

<u>1748–1813</u>

## 12 SEP 1813 • St. Charles Parish, LA, USA

| • | 12 SEP |
| --- | --- |
| **1813** | |
| AGE 70 | |

**Death of Half-Brother**

His half-brother Zenon died on September 12, 1813, in New Orleans, Louisiana, when Carlos "Charles" Laveau was 70 years old.

## Zenon Trudeau

### 1748–1813

### 12 SEP 1813 • New Orleans, Louisiana

- 6 OCT **1816** AGE 73

### Death of Half-Brother

His half-brother Charles died on October 6, 1816, in New Orleans, Louisiana, when Carlos "Charles" Laveau was 73 years old.

## Charles Trudeau dit Laveaux Surveyor General of Spanish Louisiana

### 1755–1816

### 06 Oct 1816 • New Orleans, Orleans, Louisiana, United States

- 6 OCT **1816** AGE 73

### Death

Carlos "Charles" Laveau Trudeau died on October 6, 1816, in New Orleans, Louisiana, when he was 73 years old.

**6 October 1816** • **New Orleans, Orleans, Louisiana, United States**

# References

A Companion to Latin American History - Wiley Online Library. https://onlinelibrary.wiley.com/doi/pdf/10.1002/9781444391633. Accessed 15 Aug. 2020.

A Little History of the United States - REPUBLIC OF CALLAMARI. https://republicofcallamari.weebly.com/uploads/3/8/0/7/38076783/a_little_history_of_the_united_states.pdf. Accessed 15 Aug. 2020.

A trinity of beliefs and a unity of the sacred: modern Vodou .... https://pdfs.semanticscholar.org/89f6/c17f361d0b62146ba4668578bf63b1007d09.pdf. Accessed 15 Aug. 2020.

African amulets. http://dpositive.com.ng/enb/african-amulets.html. Accessed 15 Aug. 2020.

American History Week 5 Flashcards | Quizlet. https://quizlet.com/339148012/american-history-week-5-flash-cards/. Accessed 15 Aug. 2020.

Antebellum Period - HistoryNet. https://www.historynet.com/antebellum-period. Accessed 15 Aug. 2020.

Bernardo de Galvez | 64 Parishes. https://64parishes.org/entry/bernardo-de-glvez. Accessed 27 Aug. 2020.

Black Codes and Pig Laws | Slavery By Another Name Bento | PBS. https://www.pbs.org/tpt/slavery-by-another-name/themes/black-codes/

Cajuns - 64 Parishes. https://64parishes.org/entry/cajuns. Accessed 15 Aug. 2020.

Chapter 13: Religion (ANTH 1010) Flashcards | Quizlet.
https://quizlet.com/290432641/chapter-13-religion-anth-1010-
flash-cards/. Accessed 15 Aug. 2020.

Chapter 13: Religion (ANTH 1010) Flashcards | Quizlet.
https://quizlet.com/290432641/chapter-13-religion-anth-1010-
flash-cards/. Accessed 15 Aug. 2020.

Connecting past to present Louisiana Cajuns and their sense .... 14
Feb. 2005, https://journals.openedition.org/nuevomundo/646.
Accessed 27 Aug. 2020.

Contemporary Creoleness; or, The World in Pidginization? - jstor.
https://www.jstor.org/stable/10.1086/657257. Accessed 27 Aug.
2020.

Creole | people | Britannica.
https://www.britannica.com/topic/Creole. Accessed 27 Aug. 2020.

Creole History in New Orleans - Visit New Orleans.
https://www.neworleans.com/things-to-
do/multicultural/cultures/creoles/. Accessed 15 Aug. 2020.

Creole in Louisiana - jstor. https://www.jstor.org/stable/27784777.
Accessed 15 Aug. 2020.

Creole in Louisiana - jstor. https://www.jstor.org/stable/27784777.
Accessed 27 Aug. 2020.

Creoles - History, The first creoles in america, Acculturation ....
https://www.everyculture.com/multi/Bu-Dr/Creoles.html.
Accessed 15 Aug. 2020.

Creoles | Encyclopedia.com.
https://www.encyclopedia.com/social-sciences-and-
law/anthropology-and-archaeology/people/creoles. Accessed 15
Aug. 2020.

Creoles in Louisiana History – Seventh Coalition: History. 22 Jan. 2018, https://seventhcoalition.wordpress.com/2018/01/22/creoles-in-louisiana-history/. Accessed 15 Aug. 2020.

Download Creoles And Cajuns - myq-see.com or. http://lantved.myq-see.com/509.html. Accessed 27 Aug. 2020.

Facts-on-File-Atlas-of-Hispanic-American-History.pdf. https://saalimited.com/PDFS/files/1.%20P.D.F.'s/Facts-on-File-Atlas-of-Hispanic-American-History.pdf. Accessed 15 Aug. 2020.

Frederick Gottlieb Hoberg (1826-1903) - Find A Grave Memorial. https://www.findagrave.com/memorial/37216569/frederick-gottlieb-hoberg

Free People of Color in Louisiana. https://www.lib.lsu.edu/sites/all/files/sc/fpoc/history.html

Free Blacks in the Antebellum Period - The African American .... https://www.loc.gov/exhibits/african-american-odyssey/free-blacks-in-the-antebellum-period.html. Accessed 15 Aug. 2020.

Free People of Color in Louisiana - LSU Libraries. https://lib.lsu.edu/sites/all/files/sc/fpoc/history.html. Accessed 15 Aug. 2020.

Free People of Color in the Spanish Atlantic Race and Citizenship .... https://v7.rodionblog.ru/58. Accessed 15 Aug. 2020.

Free women of color and slaveholding in New Orleans, 1810 .... https://digitalcommons.lsu.edu/cgi/viewcontent.cgi?article=4012&context=gradschool_theses. Accessed 15 Aug. 2020.

French Quarter History | Walking History Tours | Katrina and .... https://www.frenchquarter.com/history/2/. Accessed 15 Aug. 2020.

From Marie Laveau to Voodoo Festival in New Orleans. 5 Apr. 2019, http://laventurelouisianaise.blogspot.com/2019/04/from-marie-laveau-to-voodoo-festival-in.html. Accessed 15 Aug. 2020.

Haitian Immigration : Eighteenth and Nineteenth ... - AAME :. http://www.inmotionaame.org/print.cfm?migration=5. Accessed 15 Aug. 2020.

Haitian Immigration to Louisiana in the Eighteenth ... - AAME :. http://www.inmotionaame.org/texts/viewer.cfm?id=5_000T. Accessed 15 Aug. 2020.

Haitian Revolution | Causes, Summary, & Facts | Britannica. https://www.britannica.com/topic/Haitian-Revolution. Accessed 27 Aug. 2020.

Haitians: A People on the Move. Haitian Cultural Heritage .... https://files.eric.ed.gov/fulltext/ED416263.pdf. Accessed 15 Aug. 2020.

History | Los Islenos Heritage and Cultural Society. https://www.losislenos.org/history/. Accessed 27 Aug. 2020.

History of slavery in Maryland -. https://www. History_of_slavery_in_Maryland. Accessed 15 Aug. 2020.

Introduction: The Making and Unmaking of an Atlantic World .... https://www.oxfordhandbooks.com/view/10.1093/oxfordhb/9780199210879.001.0001/oxfordhb-9780199210879-e-1. Accessed 15 Aug. 2020.

JULIE YVONNE WEBB, RN, MS Hyg. Miss Webb ... - CDC stacks. https://stacks.cdc.gov/view/cdc/62808/cdc_62808_DS1.pdf?. Accessed 27 Aug. 2020.

Les Cenelles: Choix de poésies indigènes · DSCF. http://silverbox.gmu.edu/dscff/s/aaaw/item/476. Accessed 15 Aug. 2020.

Li Grand Zombi | Dieline. 13 Mar. 2013, http://www.thedieline.com/blog/2013/3/13/li-grand-zombi.html. Accessed 15 Aug. 2020.

Louisiana voodoo and superstitions related to health.. https://www.ncbi.nlm.nih.gov/pmc/articles/PMC1937133/. Accessed 27 Aug. 2020.

Marie Catherine Laveau, Voodoo Priestess (c.1801 - c.1881 .... 13 Apr. 2020, https://www.geni.com/people/Marie-Laveau-Voodoo-Priestess/6000000012337864987. Accessed 15 Aug. 2020.

Marie Glapion - Historical records and family trees - MyHeritage. https://www.myheritage.com/names/marie_glapion. Accessed 15 Aug. 2020.

Marie Laveau – WRSP - World Religions and Spirituality Project. 27 Oct. 2017, https://wrldrels.org/2017/10/27/marie-laveau/. Accessed 15 Aug. 2020.

Marie Laveau | Biography & Facts | Britannica. https://www.britannica.com/biography/Marie-Laveau. Accessed 15 Aug. 2020.

Marie Laveau | New Orleans Voodoo Queen | History. https://ghostcitytours.com/new-orleans/marie-laveau/. Accessed 15 Aug. 2020.

Marie Laveau The Voodoo Queen of New Orleans - Naked .... 20 Sep. 2015, http://www.historynaked.com/marie-laveau-voodoo-queen-new-orleans/. Accessed 15 Aug. 2020.

Marie laveau. https://divansale.com/wmr6qzd/marie-laveau.html. Accessed 15 Aug. 2020.

Midterm essay for anthropology course | Social Science .... https://www.homeworkmarket.com/files/mythritualmysticismbook -pdf-5148409. Accessed 15 Aug. 2020.

Negotiating Race and Status in Senegal, Saint Domingue .... http://www.columbia.edu/~pf3/rossignol.pdf. Accessed 15 Aug. 2020.

New Orleans City Guide 1938 - NOLA Pyrate Week. https://nolapyrateweek.com/wp-content/uploads/New_Orleans_City_Guide_1938.pdf. Accessed 15 Aug. 2020.

Pentecostalism and Witchcraft. https://link.springer.com/content/pdf/10.1007%2F978-3-319-56068-7.pdf. Accessed 27 Aug. 2020.

Political and Economic History of Haiti - San Jose State .... https://www.sjsu.edu/faculty/watkins/haiti.htm. Accessed 27 Aug. 2020.

Racial and Ethnic Groups in the Gulf of Mexico Region: Cajuns. https://www.lsuagcenter.com/~/media/system/c/1/6/3/c163dd4e4df c692ac2bd44060c49a0df/rr118racialandethnicgroupsinthegulfofme xicoregionc.pdf. Accessed 27 Aug. 2020.


Racial and Ethnic Groups in the Gulf of Mexico Region: Cajuns. https://www.lsuagcenter.com/~/media/system/c/1/6/3/c163dd4e4df c692ac2bd44060c49a0df/rr118racialandethnicgroupsinthegulfofme xicoregionc.pdf. Accessed 27 Aug. 2020.


Religion, History and the Supreme Gods of Africa: A ... - jstor.

https://www.jstor.org/stable/1581452. Accessed 27 Aug. 2020.

Slaveholding free women of color in antebellum New Orleans ....
https://digitalcommons.lsu.edu/cgi/viewcontent.cgi?article=4071&
context=gradschool_dissertations. Accessed 15 Aug. 2020.

Slavery in Spanish Colonial Louisiana | 64 Parishes.
https://64parishes.org/entry/slavery-in-spanish-colonial-louisiana.
Accessed 27 Aug. 2020.

Slavery in the Colonial Louisiana Backcountry - jstor.
https://www.jstor.org/stable/23074684. Accessed 15 Aug. 2020.

Slavery in the Colonies | Boundless US History.
https://courses.lumenlearning.com/boundless-
ushistory/chapter/slavery-in-the-colonies/. Accessed 15 Aug. 2020.

Slavery in the United States - EH.net.
https://eh.net/encyclopedia/slavery-in-the-united-states/. Accessed
15 Aug. 2020.

Slavery in the United States - EH.net.
https://eh.net/encyclopedia/slavery-in-the-united-states/. Accessed
15 Aug. 2020.

Social Classification in Creole Louisiana - jstor.
https://www.jstor.org/stable/643621. Accessed 15 Aug. 2020.

Social Classification in Creole Louisiana - jstor.
https://www.jstor.org/stable/643621. Accessed 15 Aug. 2020.

Southern Folk Artist & Antiques Dealer/Collector: "Créole
Soirée". 26 Jun. 2016,
http://andrewhopkinsart.blogspot.com/2016/06/creole-soiree.html.
Accessed 15 Aug. 2020.

Spanish Colonial Louisiana | 64 Parishes.

https://64parishes.org/entry/spanish-colonial-louisiana. Accessed 15 Aug. 2020.

Spanish legacy continues | People | iberianet.com. 22 Apr. 2018, https://www.iberianet.com/people/spanish-legacy-continues/article_85227f96-4509-11e8-b57a-7b134aea67cb.html. Accessed 27 Aug. 2020.

The "Nous" of Southern Catholic Quadroons: Racial, Ethnic .... https://www.researchgate.net/publication/31018177_The_Nous_of_Southern_Catholic_Quadroons_Racial_Ethnic_and_Religious_Identity_in_Les_Cenelles. Accessed 15 Aug. 2020.

The African American Experience in Louisiana. 15 May. 2012, https://www.crt.state.la.us/Assets/OCD/hp/nationalregister/historic_contexts/The_African_American_Experience_in_Louisiana.pdf. Accessed 27 Aug. 2020.

The African American heritage of Florida. https://ufdc.ufl.edu/AA00061985/00001. Accessed 15 Aug. 2020.

The Black Auxiliary Troops of King Carlos IV - Vanderbilt's .... 17 May. 2015, https://etd.library.vanderbilt.edu/available/etd-05172015-181542/unrestricted/MiriamMartinErickson.pdf. Accessed 15 Aug. 2020.

The Catholic Voodoo Queen and the Demonization of New .... https://digitalcommons.chapman.edu/cgi/viewcontent.cgi?article=1106&context=vocesnovae. Accessed 27 Aug. 2020.

The Domestic Slave Trade - AAME :. http://www.inmotionaame.org/print.cfm?migration=3. Accessed 15 Aug. 2020.

The education of louisiana's gens de couleur libres ... - Core. https://core.ac.uk/download/pdf/158321730.pdf. Accessed 15 Aug. 2020.

The Encyclopedia of Witches, Witchcraft and Wicca - Semantic ....
1 Mar. 2020,
https://pdfs.semanticscholar.org/5873/43e3cc13020a3e417282e159
c2c79db219ed.pdf. Accessed 15 Aug. 2020.

The european - World history.
http://www.worldhistory.biz/download567/TheAmericanIndians-
TheEuropeanChallenge(History%20Ebook)_worldhistory.biz.pdf.
Accessed 15 Aug. 2020.

The Free People of Color in Louisiana and St. Domingue: A ....
https://www.jstor.org/stable/3786302. Accessed 15 Aug. 2020.

The House on Bayou Road: Atlantic Creole Networks in ... - jstor.
https://www.jstor.org/stable/44308570. Accessed 15 Aug. 2020.

The National and Cultural Groups of New Orleans - Folklife in ....
http://www.louisianafolklife.org/lt/virtual_books/guide_to_state/N
OGroups.html. Accessed 27 Aug. 2020.

 The New Orleans Free People of Color and the Process of ....
https://scholarworks.wm.edu/cgi/viewcontent.cgi?article=6491&co
ntext=etd. Accessed 15 Aug. 2020.

 The New Orleans Free People of Color and the Process of ....
https://scholarworks.wm.edu/cgi/viewcontent.cgi?article=6491&co
ntext=etd. Accessed 15 Aug. 2020.

The New Orleans Free People of Color and the Process of ....
https://scholarworks.wm.edu/cgi/viewcontent.cgi?article=6491&co
ntext=etd. Accessed 27 Aug. 2020.


The Portuguese and the Creole Indian Ocean Essays in Historical
.... https://ii.metaldoor12.ru/141. Accessed 15 Aug. 2020.

The Slave Trade and the Ethnic Diversity of Louisiana's ... - jstor.

https://www.jstor.org/stable/4233285. Accessed 27 Aug. 2020.

The Story of French New Orleans History of a Creole City. https://t7.smoloblvetlab.ru/3. Accessed 15 Aug. 2020.

The True History and Faith Behind Voodoo - French Quarter. https://www.frenchquarter.com/true-history-faith-behind-voodoo/. Accessed 15 Aug. 2020.

The Voodoo Hoodoo Spellbook - MetaphysicSpirit.com. http://www.metaphysicspirit.com/books/The%20Voodoo%20Hood oo%20Spellbook.pdf. Accessed 15 Aug. 2020.

The Voodoo Hoodoo Spellbook: Li Grand Zombi. http://voodoohoodoospellbook.blogspot.com/p/serpent-worship.html. Accessed 15 Aug. 2020.

The Voodoo Queen, the Cheerleader, and the ... - Nouvelle. https://c.nouvelle-ug.ru/26. Accessed 15 Aug. 2020.

This is the difference between Cajun and Creole - 10Best. 20 Mar. 2018, https://www.10best.com/interests/food-culture/this-is-the-difference-between-cajun-and-creole/. Accessed 27 Aug. 2020.

Voodoo - rituals, world, burial, body, life, beliefs, time .... http://www.deathreference.com/Vi-Z/Voodoo.html

Voodoo dictionary definition | voodoo defined - YourDictionary. https://www.yourdictionary.com/voodoo. Accessed 27 Aug. 2020.

Voodoo in louisiana - Core. https://core.ac.uk/download/pdf/295552849.pdf. Accessed 27 Aug. 2020.

Voodoo priestess new orleans. http://mcbpc20088.nichost.ru/rsvc/voodoo-priestess-new-orleans.html. Accessed 15 Aug. 2020.

Voodoo Religions: Beliefs & Rituals - Video & Lesson ....
https://study.com/academy/lesson/voodoo-religions-beliefs-
rituals.html. Accessed 15 Aug. 2020.

Voodoo Religions: Beliefs & Rituals - Video & Lesson ....
https://study.com/academy/lesson/voodoo-religions-beliefs-
rituals.html. Accessed 15 Aug. 2020.

What does che mean in creole - Key Route Lofts #101.
http://keyroutelofts101.com/site/2a1ei.php?0c08af=what-does-che-
mean-in-creole. Accessed 15 Aug. 2020.

What Is Louisiana Voodoo Really All About Anyway?. 18 Jul.
2016, https://wheninyourstate.com/louisiana/what-is-that-voodoo-
that-you-do/. Accessed 15 Aug. 2020.

What's the Difference Between Cajun and Creole? - TripSavvy. 28
May. 2019, https://www.tripsavvy.com/the-difference-between-
cajun-and-creole-3961097. Accessed 27 Aug. 2020.

# ABOUT THE AUTHOR

The author has a B.S. degree from the University of Arkansas, Pine Bluff Arkansas, B.R. E. in Religious Education from Carver Baptist College and Seminary, Kansas City, Missouri, Masters of Art in History, Masters of Divinity, D. Min. with a focus on Global Health and Wellness from the Saint Paul School of Theology, Leawood, Kansas, Ph.D. in Counseling, Trinity College of Bible and Theological Seminary, Certification in Community Health Worker, Metropolitan Community College, Kansas City, Missouri, Received 75 doctoral hours in Organizational Leadership with a focus on Behavior Health from Grand Canyon University, Phoenix, Arizona. The auther served as a chaplain, adjunct professor of Philosophy and Religion, ESL (English as a Second Language) and medical educator. The author enjoys history, ancestry, and genealogy.

Made in the USA
Middletown, DE
24 September 2023

39227759R00082